A Call *to*
PRAYER

INTERCESSION
in ACTION

by
Germaine Copeland

Harrison House
Tulsa, Oklahoma

A Call to Prayer—
Intercession in Action
ISBN 1-57794-327-9

ISBN 0-89274-855-9
(Revised, formerly ISBN 0-89274-440-5, copyright © 1987)

05 04 03 02   10 8 7 6 5 4 3

Copyright © 2001 by Germaine Copeland
Word Ministries, Inc.
38 Sloan Street
Roswell, Georgia 30075
www.prayers.org

Published by Harrison House, Inc.
P.O. Box 35035
Tulsa, Oklahoma 74153

Front Cover Image © Corbis Stock Market/Craig Tuttle/2001

And this is the confidence that we have in him, that, if we ask anything according to his will, he heareth us: and if we know that he hear us, whatsoever we ask, we know that we have the petitions that we desired of him.

1 John 5:14,15 KJV

Dedication

This book is dedicated to Rev. A.H. "Buck" Griffin, my Dad
and
Donnis Brock Griffin, my Mom who is in heaven.
They were my mentors who prayed with us each morning
and evening, teaching us that God answers prayer.

Contents

Acknowledgments

*I*f I were to acknowledge everyone who has helped me in my search for knowledge on intercessory prayer, the list of names would be quite lengthy. I will name a few who encouraged and supported me, read the manuscript, critiqued, made valuable suggestions and prayed for me. Donna Walker, my editor and friend at Word Ministries, was the first to read the scrawled yellow sheets of paper and assured me that I have a God-given ability to write. I thank Pat Horton, another member of the Word Ministries team, and the many others who have requested the reprinting of this work. A big "thank you" to Andrell Stevens, editor for Harrison House, who recognized the value of this work and assisted us in updating and rewriting. I thank Everette, my husband, for exercising much patience during the writing and rewriting of this manuscript.

Prayer is an inexhaustible subject. There is always more to learn. Since the original printing of this work in 1987 many have helped shape my prayer life. Thank you, Holy Spirit, for leading me and directing me in the practical application of God's Word as I continue developing a lifestyle of prayer.

Introduction

Intercessory prayer is prayer offered on behalf of another person (or other persons) as an expression of love. Jesus said, Greater love hath no man than this, that a man lay down his life for his friends (John 15:13 KJV). Intercession is a manifestation of that God-kind of love.

In Ephesians 6:12 KJV we discover that, as Christians, *we wrestle not against flesh and blood, but against principalities, against powers, against the rulers of the darkness of this world, against spiritual wickedness in high places.* God provided a tested and proven armor for us to wear in this spiritual walk and He provided the necessary weapons to successfully destroy those strongholds where Satan makes his last stand. We are prepared to pray in the Spirit on every occasion with all kinds of prayer. This armor is the same prayer armor that Jesus wore when He came to earth as the Intercessor for all mankind (Isa. 59:16,17).

God has called the church to pray for all the saints and for all men everywhere (Eph. 6:18; 1 Tim. 2:1).

This book is written to encourage intercessory prayer, and to influence believers to look to the Word of God for sound doctrine, reproof, correction and instruction (2 Tim. 3:16).

The different kinds of prayers mentioned in the Bible are practiced in this ministry as the Holy Spirit continues to teach us to pray "prayers that avail much" (James 5:16).

It is imperative that we know God, know who we are in Christ and know our enemy. Our archenemy understands the importance of prayer and works diligently to rob us of time and energy that we give to praying. Remember, there is no distance in the spirit world. That prayer you offer up in your present location can strike like lightning in another part of the world, bringing about the plan and purpose of God.

When you begin to pray for others, you become a part of the present-day ministry of Jesus Christ, *seeing he ever liveth to make intercession* (Heb. 7:25 KJV). Through prayer, you and I become His voice in the earth. With the help of the Holy Spirit, we become laborers with our heavenly Father.

Intercession begins with an act of an individual's will in obedience to God the Father and is a spiritual exercise. The two most valuable tools in intercession are: (1) the Word of God, and (2) prayer in the spirit.

And this is the confidence that we have in him
[God], *that, if we ask any thing according to*
his will, he heareth us: and if we know that
he hear us, whatsoever we ask, we know that
we have the petitions that we desired of him.

1 John 5:14,15 KJV

God's will is His Word. The Word of God is spirit and it brings life. Praying in other tongues is praying in the language of the spirit rather than in the language of the mind. It moves the person out of the natural (physical) realm into the supernatural (spiritual) realm. This enables him to pray beyond his own limited human knowledge as he gives voice to the Holy Spirit within him. The Spirit of the Lord is then free to bear the intercessor up to express the mind and will of God through him and to help him produce supernatural results.

Since the Holy Spirit knows the will and plan of God, He can assist you when you pray in tongues by helping you to hold and express the thoughts, feelings and purposes of God's own heart. By cooperating with the Holy Spirit, you enable Him to aid you in praying for the fulfillment of God's purpose. When you pray in the spirit, you are speaking to God concerning divine secrets.

You may proclaim with the apostle Paul, *I will pray with the spirit, and I will pray with the under-*

standing [the mind] *also* (1 Cor. 14:15 KJV). That is God's overall scriptural plan for effective prayer.

It is my intention in these pages to share with you some insights the Holy Spirit has taught me over the past several years about this subject of prayer. The instruction in this book applies both to individual prayers of positive confession and intercession, as well as to group prayers of this type.

Even though I share some truths with you in this book, the only way you will ever really learn about prayer is to actively get involved in it yourself. It is then that your personal Teacher and Guide, the Holy Spirit, can begin to give you wisdom and spiritual understanding in this vital area.

When I first made a decision to act on God's Word concerning prayer, it was an overwhelming project. At that time my family was experiencing a crisis situation in our home, which could only be set right by divine intervention. God looked for someone "who would build up the wall and stand in the gap before Him for the land (our family) that He should not destroy it" (Ezek. 22:30). From that experience I learned that not only does God tell us in His Word *how* to pray, He also tells us *who* is called to pray and *the way* to enter into this important phase of ministry.

This is the practical, spiritual knowledge that I would like to share with you in this book.

1

Forms of Intercession

What is intercession? It involves the lifting up in prayer of another person and is manifested in various forms. However, whatever form it may take, it is imperative that our intercession places us in agreement with God. We establish this agreement with the Lord by articulating His Word. Through the words of the apostle Paul, our Father has given instruction in 1 Timothy 2:1-2 KJV for the kinds of prayer methods that will assure us a quiet and peaceable life, which is His will for us.

I exhort therefore, that, first of all, supplications, prayers, intercessions, and giving of thanks, be made for all men; for kings, and for all that are in authority; that we may lead a quiet and peaceable life in all godliness and honesty.

As Christians we are to involve ourselves in the affairs of God and humanity through intercession. In the name of Jesus, we come boldly before the throne of grace, approaching God in faith and confidence, addressing Him in familiar but respectful conversational language, asking that His will be done on earth as it is in heaven. In order to converse with God, we must learn to speak as God speaks, because we are told that if we ask anything according to His will, He hears us (1 John 5:14,15). To know God's will, we must study and know His written Word. His will is revealed to us in His Word—so His will *is* His Word.

Our confidence toward God is strong when we know what *He* says about the situations for which we are praying. He has given us the mind of Christ. He has also provided us with His written Word so that His mind can be developed within us as we read, study and meditate upon the Scriptures.

For instance, let's look at what the Bible has to say about the will of God for humankind. First Timothy 2:4 tells us that God wishes for all men to be saved, and to come into the full knowledge of the truth. Therefore, we can pray for the salvation of others, in full confidence that by so doing we are praying in agreement with the Word and will of God. Then we can be assured: (1) that the Lord of the harvest hears our prayer (1 John 5:14); (2) that He will send forth laborers into His harvest fields who will share the Good News of the Gospel with the lost (Matt. 9:38); and (3) that those who hear and believe will be delivered from the authority of darkness and translated into the kingdom of God's dear Son (Col. 1:13).

After we pray for all men, we can then pray the following prayer for those in authority over us:

> Father, I intercede on behalf of those in positions of authority, seeking Your intervention in the affairs of their lives and our country. Thank You for the freedom we enjoy. I ask You to direct our decisions at the voting polls that we may elect the uncompromisingly righteous to be in positions of authority so that we can rejoice. I ask You to establish their offices that they will be made secure by righteousness. Cause righteous and just lips to be a delight to those in authority that they may love those who speak what is right. In the name of Jesus I pray. Amen.

Praying in the Spirit

Many people never experience the depth of this second phase of intercession because of wrong teaching, fear or lack of knowledge. In Romans 8:26-27 NKJV we read:

> *Likewise the Spirit also helps in our weaknesses. For we do not know what we should*

*pray for as we ought, but the Spirit Himself
makes intercession for us with groanings
which cannot be uttered.*

He searches the hearts and knows what the mind of the Spirit is, because He makes intercession for the saints according to the will of God.

When you do not know how to pray about a certain situation, that is the appropriate time to use your prayer language–to pray in a tongue that is unknown to your natural mind. When you have exhausted your conscious knowledge of the situation, there is still Someone who knows every aspect of the case. He also knows the mind of the Father in a way that is far above and beyond your natural understanding. Your praying in the Spirit– in an unknown tongue–enables the Holy Spirit to assist you in achieving His desired results.

Let me share with you an experience that I believe will help to illustrate this "deeper level" of intercession.

One day as I was praying for a certain minister, I began by saying, "Father, I don't know how to pray for this man according to the prophecies that have been spoken concerning him, and I don't know anything else to pray." (Have you ever been in that situation?) Then, after a short time of praying in the Spirit, I was aware that the Spirit of God was helping me to pray. I was uttering heartrending sobs in a language that I had never expressed before in prayer.

After an interval of time, I began to pray in my natural language, English. As I listened, I found myself saying (again by the Spirit of God), "Father, I thank You that this man is not ready to be offered up, that his time of departure is not at hand, that it is only after the fulfillment of all prophecies that he will say, 'I have fought a good fight, I have finished my course, I have kept the faith.' Then, Father, he will receive the crown of righteousness which You have laid up for him on that day."

Then I began to rejoice in God my Redeemer, laughing, clapping and dancing about. Later, I found out that this minister believed that he was finished, that no one wanted to hear what he had to say, that there was no longer a place for him in the body of Christ.

Only the Spirit of God could have known these things. It was the Holy Spirit who was searching out the heart of this individual and who also knew the plan of God for him. While the enemy was working against him with thoughts contrary to the will of God, the Spirit of the Lord was working on his behalf through someone who responded to the call to pray. Through this cooperative intercession between a willing believer and the Holy Spirit, the strategy and plan of the enemy was exposed and thwarted.

Praying in Travail

Another form of intercession is travail. Even though some people do not believe that travail is necessary, in his letter to the Galatian saints Paul writes, *My little children, of whom I travail in birth again until Christ be formed in you* (Gal. 4:19 KJV). Here Paul intimates that he had previously travailed for their spiritual birth, and he is now travailing once again for their spiritual development and maturity.

Let's explore this passage of Scripture. The Greek word translated *travail* in this verse is *odino,* a verb meaning "to experience the pains of birth."[1] In this context, travail is a spiritual activity. Its purpose is to "bring forth" or to "give birth." As in natural childbirth, we cannot will spiritual travail to take place, nor can we "work it up," as many have tried to do. Travail is not a product of the mind, will or emotions.

The prophet Isaiah foretold of the coming Messiah: *He* [God] *shall see the travail of his* [Jesus'] *soul, and shall be satisfied* (Isa. 53:11 KJV). Jesus was the Intercessor whom God required to suffer the birth pains of redemption for all mankind. God had searched everywhere for a human intercessor and could not find one, so He assumed the responsibility Himself in the form of His Son.

The legal side of redemption was provided for in the death and resurrection of God's Anointed. Today you and I are living on the vital side of redemption. Travail has not passed away, for people will not be saved unless someone on earth prays. Through the means of prayer God delivers them out of the authority of darkness and translates them into the kingdom of God's dear Son. Right now, Jesus is seated at the right hand of God the Father in heaven, interceding for humanity. This intercession is released into the earth through His body of believers, just as spiritual endowments are released through the believers as the Spirit wills.

As servants of Christ, our first priority in prayer is the salvation of mankind, followed by "travail in birth until Christ be formed in them," bringing deliverance and full maturity. Travail is not a "flaky" manifestation of the flesh, but true travail originates with the Holy Spirit and emanates from the spirit of the intercessor.

Travail is often a subject debated among the churches. My viewpoint is this: let those who travail, travail, and let those who don't, don't. Let's not allow the church of Jesus Christ to split over this issue.

Travail usually comes forth with groanings and moanings too deep to be uttered in articulate speech (Rom. 8:26). Travail is of the spirit, from the Holy Spirit, and not of the flesh (human nature). However, the flesh (the human mind, will and emotions) can be affected by an individual's interpretation of the travail process or by his level of spiritual understanding and maturity.

Privately (or in group prayer, in which each intercessor has knowledge and understanding of travail), an individual is free to respond physically and emotionally to the workings of the Holy Spirit by yielding to Him his entire being–spirit, soul and body. However, in public we must exercise extreme self-control in this area.

We govern, or hold in check, our human emotions and physical responses. The mistake that has been made in the past is that those who have placed their confidence in physical or emotional manifestations have attempted to *initiate* a work of the Spirit by crying, screaming, shaking or moaning. Those I have talked with say they cannot stop this physical or emotional activity. They believe that they are submitted to a spiritual force greater than themselves and their behavior is beyond their control.

In 1 Corinthians 14:32 the apostle Paul reminds us that the spirit of a prophet is subject to the prophet. I believe that the spirit of the intercessor is subject to the intercessor. *The Holy Spirit does not "overpower" anyone against His will, nor does He work in a manner to call undue attention to any person or group of people.* His job is to glorify Jesus Christ.

God's Holy Spirit is not repulsive; He does not drive other people away from Jesus through strange or bizarre activity. When we read the Gospels, we realize that there were times Jesus acted in ways that we might consider odd, such as writing on the ground with His finger (John 8:6,7) and making mud with His saliva and spreading it on a man's eyes (John 9:6). We can't rule out the move of the Spirit on certain individuals that may look strange to us, but we can ask, "Is this behavior drawing people to Jesus?"

Travail is a cry before the Father and should be done in the prayer closet or with those who have understanding in the area of intercession. Travail emanates from the spirit of an individual at the impulse of the Holy Spirit; it cannot be "worked up"! In general public worship, you should exercise the self-control that has been given to you by God the Father (2 Tim. 1:7).

I have experienced and observed travail in desperate circumstances. One night as I was praying with a friend, she began to travail with a fervor which could not be expressed except in cries and moans. As she travailed, I prayed in the Spirit. Through a word of knowledge, the Holy Spirit revealed to us the identity of the couple for whom she was interceding and that they were in grave danger; it was a life-or-death situation. After a short period of time, my prayer partner was released from the travail, and the peace of God that surpasses understanding consumed each of us–spirit, soul and body. This peace ushered us into the rest of God. Deliverance had been brought forth and completed (Heb. 4:11).

Later, we learned that on that very day the husband for whom we had been praying had acquired a pistol for the purpose of killing his wife and himself. Satan's plan was thwarted when two people responded to the call to pray, and deliverance was birthed for those who did not know how to go to God for themselves. The call to prayer was released in the hearts of believers who responded to the prompting of the Holy Spirit.

If you are searching for your ministry, begin here– by giving yourself to others through intercessory prayer. Let's not allow the art of intercession to be lost, or stolen from us, through ignorance and neglect. In His Word, God tells us that He will not allow our foot to be caught in a trap or hidden snare (Prov. 3:26). His light will dispel the darkness if we are willing to learn from one another. Many hurts and costly mistakes can be avoided if we heed the counsel and advice of those who have walked this way before.

Let's be intercessors. Let's learn to "pray one for another," as our Lord has instructed (James 5:16).

2

Purpose of Intercession

The purpose of intercession is to establish the will of the Father on the earth. God's purpose far outreaches the comprehension of the average churchgoer. However, within the broad scope of His plan we can approach the Father on behalf of others, praying as He has instructed us, in order that we may lead a quiet and peaceable life and influence the lives of others. Through the medium of prayer we are instrumental in establishing the intercession of Jesus on the earth.

Spirit-Led Intercession Brings Deliverance

One day as I sat down in my den to pray, I felt overwhelmed by the many and various needs of numerous individuals. There were too many names to even mention. As I sat there contemplating how and where to start, I said aloud: "Father, I do not know where to begin today. There are so many needs in the world. You know where intercession is most needed at this moment. I present my body to You as a living sacrifice, holy and acceptable unto You, which is my reasonable service and spiritual worship, to pray for whomever You will. Jesus is searching the hearts and, Holy Spirit, according to Romans 8, You know the plan of God for today."

All of the Godhead is searching our hearts and the hearts of others. If you and I are willing, the Holy Spirit can bring us alongside another who needs spiritual assistance. The Spirit knows the very spot of the heaviest enemy attack and whose heart is crying out for freedom (Rom. 8:26,27).

I began to pray in the Spirit, and after praying for a few minutes, I realized that I was entering into that arena of prayer where the Holy Spirit "takes hold together with us" against our infirmities—our inability to produce results (Rom. 8:26). I did not even know for whom I was praying, much less the desired results.

In order for you to really appreciate this experience, I need to tell you that for a period of time after our son David was delivered from a life of drugs and all that goes with it, he returned to his old habits. When I realized that he was on drugs again, I said: "Lord, for seven years I believed for that boy's release. I saw him set free after he read the book of Malachi from *The Living Bible* while sitting in his own living room all alone—just he and the Holy Ghost. He has given his testimony and witnessed for You, and now he is bringing a reproach to the body of Christ. I am through. You will have to raise up another intercessor this time."

(It does not pay to tell God what you will and will not do. Aren't you glad that God looks on the heart? Through this experience I learned that He has a keen sense of humor.)

As I continued to pray in the Spirit, I found myself standing before a building. It was obviously a business, and I recognized where I was because I had been there before. When I walked around the building I saw him—David. There he stood, engrossed in his work. He was totally unaware of three demonic spirits around his head. One had his fingers in David's ears, another had his hands over David's eyes and the third had his arm around David's head as though he were binding something to his mind.

In my boldness, these three presented no problem to me. I was in the Spirit and knew that I had been given authority over all the power of the satanic kingdom. I began to speak to those spirits, and when they heard my voice they became very agitated. As I gave them the command to go in the name of Jesus, they left one by one. It was then that I began to pray in English as the Holy Spirit gave me utterance, ministering deliverance, peace and restoration to David's inner man.

When I turned to leave, I saw one of those demons peeking around the corner of the building. I stamped my foot and repeated the command for it to go in the name of Jesus and not to return, and it left. It was then that I realized that physically I was still in my home.

A few days later, when I talked with David, I asked him if God had been talking to him recently. He shared with me how he had not wanted the other guys to feel that he was self-righteous and had yielded once again to smoking pot. He believed that he could "walk in the middle of the road," remaining a Christian, yet taking a smoke when he wanted one—after all, he could handle it now.

This kind of thinking is a snare of the enemy into which many Christians have fallen because of a lack of knowledge. David admitted, however, that lately he had become concerned because he realized that he was no longer hearing the voice of God. He continued:

"I woke up the other morning and saw that I was no longer in the middle of the road. I was not only over on the side, but I was off the shoulder and into the ditch. I had been confused about the voices that I was hearing and was no longer sure about what was true.

This morning I heard God's voice and knew that it was the Lord speaking to me. I heard and understood the truth."

Praise the name of Jesus, I saw the purpose of intercession in action when I cooperated with the Holy Spirit in prayer. Deliverance and restoration were accomplished—the prodigal son had come home. Yes, the Holy Spirit knew where the intercession was most needed that day. The result was the establishment of God's will on "the earth," the life of our son.

Pleading the Cause of Others

Pleading the cause of others, as in a court case, is another purpose of intercession (1 Tim. 2:1). Here again, Jesus is our example. Isaiah said of Him, *He bare the sin of many, and made intercession for the transgressors* (Isa. 53:12 KJV).

When praying for others, it is important to unite with the Spirit. There is power in our words, and if we do not pray according to the will of God, we will pray amiss, perhaps delaying or thwarting the fulfillment of God's plan and purpose in the individual's life.

It is imperative that we have the intercession of Jesus revealed to us for those with whom we are emotionally involved, especially our loved ones. This is an area in which our own will and feelings can so easily come into play. When we react emotionally to a situation, allowing pride or emotions to control us, the picture becomes distorted and we may lose a sense of the proper manner in which to pray; sometimes we may even find ourselves seeking revenge in certain situations.

Intercession as Defense or Vindication

Another purpose of intercession is to defend or vindicate someone or his actions. We cannot do this while holding anything against the person for whom we are praying. In order to pray for others, we must forgive. Unforgiveness is the primary hindrance to answered prayer.

There was a period of time when I was having difficulty praying for one of our daughters. She had been saved at an early age; later, in her teenage years she was filled with the Holy Spirit. Since the time of her salvation, she had faithfully read her Bible. After she graduated from college, she was different, and I did not like what I was seeing.

While she was still in high school, God performed a miracle in our relationship. We had experienced a communication breakdown. The Spirit of God taught me how to pray for her. I wrote that prayer down and prayed it until the breakthrough came.[1]

Not only were her attitudes changed, but God also taught me more about working out my own salvation with fear and trembling and, as a result, godly changes took place within me.

This was the daughter who had prayed for her mom and dad when we were having a communication problem which looked hopeless: "Jesus is Mom and Dad's peace, and He has made both one and has broken down the middle wall of partition between them. He has abolished in His flesh the enmity, to make in Himself of the two, one new man, so making peace. He has reconciled both unto God in one body by the cross, having slain the enmity thereby" (Eph. 2:14-16).

She shared this prayer with me, and we prayed in agreement knowing that Jesus said, *"If two of you on earth agree about anything you ask for, it will be done for you by my Father in heaven"* (Matt. 18:19 NIV).

It appeared now, after college, that in her pursuit of money and pleasure, our daughter had forsaken all that we had taught her and that God had very little space in her life. I began praying for her, but apparently to no avail.

One day my husband said to me: "You have grown very hard toward Terri, and you are holding things against her. You need to forgive her and continue walking in love."

At first I refused to believe this was true, but God by His Spirit revealed to me that in order for my prayers on her behalf to have any effect, I had to acknowledge my unforgiveness and repent. He reminded me of John 20:23 NIV: "*If you forgive anyone his sins, they are forgiven; if you do not forgive them, they are not forgiven.*" I had never known how to apply this Scripture and was concerned about praying presumptuously or foolishly. It was my heart's desire to pray accurately and according to the intercession of Jesus.

First, I asked forgiveness for my attitude toward my daughter, and God was faithful and just to forgive me and cleanse me from all unrighteousness (1 John 1:9). Then the Holy Spirit led me to release her from her sins. I certainly did not want my child suffering the judgment pronounced on sin. I wanted her delivered. Words began to come forth in English: "Father, I forgive her, and according to Your Word, her sins are forgiven. I no longer hold anything against her, and according to Your Word, neither do You."

Now, I do not spend very much time talking to the devil, but I do so when it is necessary for him to understand that I am aware of his position in relation to me and the situation for which I am praying. So I told him firmly:

"Satan, you cannot have our daughter nor destroy her. You will not bring affliction upon her. I suppress the judgment that is attached to sin and declare that she is forgiven. I am now standing in the gap until she comes to her senses and personal repentance. She is part of our household and a partaker of the blood covenant."

Then I loosed her from the deception and lies of the enemy and released to her "godly sorrow which produces repentance unto salvation that she "might receive life and that more abundantly" (2 Cor. 7:10; John 10:10). Then it was time to rejoice and give glory to God for His intervention in her life. She did awake to righteousness and return to the Shepherd of her soul. Glory to God for the great things that He has done.

Intercession in Accordance With God's Will

Our prayers must be in accordance with God's purpose and plan. There was a time when Judah had committed the sin of idolatry. God told Jeremiah that he was not to pray for Judah, neither was he to lift up a cry for them nor make intercession for them (Jer. 7:16).

Later, Jeremiah did intercede on their behalf, but his prayer was never answered.

There were times when God looked for a man to pray in order that He might withhold His judgment, but it seems that it was not the will of the Father to withhold His judgment from Judah at this time.

In 1 John 5:16-17 KJV, John writes:

If any man see his brother sin a sin which is not unto death, he shall ask, and he shall give him life for them that sin not unto death. There is a sin unto death: I do not say that he shall pray for it.

All unrighteousness is sin: and there is a sin not unto death.

We must know the voice of the Holy Spirit and allow Him to lead us in our prayers. We can't just get upset with people and decide that we will withhold our intercession for them because we want to see them punished.

Recompense to no man evil for evil.
Vengeance is mine; I will repay, saith the Lord.

Romans 12:17,19 KJV

The joyous intercessor is always ready to release the mercy cry, *Father, forgive them; for they know not what they do* (Luke 23:34 KJV).

Commending Others to God

In intercession you may commend others to God, as in Hebrews 7:25 and Romans 8:26-28. We commend to the Lord our loved ones, as well as others, for salvation, healing, reconciliation and restoration. In intercessory prayer we furnish any kind of assistance or help necessary to establish the eternal plan of God on the earth, being profitable to His kingdom, positively affecting individuals, communities and nations.

Intercession and God's Eternal Plan

God's overall plan includes the restoration of all things, the manifestation of the sons of God and the fulfillment of His promises to Israel (Rom. 8-11).

"The age of grace," which is also known as "the age of the Gentiles," is approaching its completion. Soon there will be the catching away of the saints, which is called "the Rapture," when we shall see Him as He is. A period of seven years of tribulation will follow, to be consummated at the second advent of Jesus Christ when He returns to earth with His saints. At that time He will establish the kingdom of heaven in this earthly realm and *the government shall be upon his shoulder* (Isa. 9:6). Israel as a nation will recognize the Messiah, Jerusalem will be His capital and God's promises to Israel will be fulfilled (Isa. 2:3). The saints will reign with Him, and Israel will become priests of the Lord to all other nations.

> *And when all things shall be subdued unto him, then shall the Son also himself be subject unto him that put all things under him, that God may be all in all.*

> 1 Corinthians 15:28 KJV

God's purposes are eternal. We are preparing the way of the Lord as He sets the stage for the millennial reign of Christ.

> *O the depth of the riches both of the wisdom and knowledge of God! how unsearchable are his judgments, and his ways past finding out! For who hath known the mind of the Lord? or who hath been his counsellor? Or who hath first given to him, and it shall be recompensed unto him again? For of him, and through him, and to him, are all things: to whom be glory for ever. Amen.*

> Romans 11:33-36 KJV

It is imperative that we continue in faith, cooperating with God's plan, praying always without fainting or turning coward. God's eternal plan will be consummated.

We must remember that it is not people we are to act against; it is the devil and his demons. In J.B. Phillips' translation of Ephesians 6:11-12 Paul writes:

Put on God's complete armour so that you can successfully resist all the devil's craftiness.

For our fight is not against any physical enemy: it is against organizations and powers that are spiritual. We are up against the unseen power that controls this dark world, and spiritual agents from the very headquarters of evil.

Our enemies, against whom we wrestle in the spiritual realm, are not flesh and blood. Do not approach God with accusations against your brothers and sisters; they are not your enemies. *To pray against any other human being, even our worst enemy, is to misuse the prayer of intercession.*

Under the old covenant, King David considered the enemies of God to be his own personal enemies, and he physically annihilated as many of them as possible. The Old Testament way of dealing with those who opposed God was to execute God's vengeance and wrath upon them. The New Testament saint administers his God-given authority in the spiritual realm, not the physical, being aware of the enemy's devices.

Let the high praises of God be in your mouth, and a two-edged sword in your hand to execute vengeance only upon the satanic kingdom (Ps. 149:6,7). Use intercessory prayer as a spiritual weapon on behalf of those held in bondage by the powers of darkness.

3

Godly Wisdom for Intercession

Art or Idol?

Some churches today are in danger of making an "idol" out of intercession and thereby losing the "art" of intercessory prayer. Some have given intercessors a status above all the fivefold ministry gifts: apostles, prophets, evangelists, pastors and teachers. Many of God's people are looking to the intercessor for leadership and guidance, expecting him or her individually (or as a group) to replace the ministry, the Word of God or even the Holy Spirit.

One church I visited had provided badges to identify their intercessors. It appeared to me that they were esteemed a notch above everyone else—including the pastor! An importance was being placed on human individuals rather than on the person of Jesus Christ, to whom it rightfully belongs. I had the distinct impression that the members of that church had forgotten the words of Paul, who said we are called *with an holy calling, not according to our works, but according to his own purpose and grace, which was given us in Christ Jesus before the world began* (2 Tim. 1:9 KJV).

At the other extreme, some pastors today are shying away from everyone who claims to be an intercessor. Many unfortunate, sad and regrettable encounters have taken place between pastors and the intercessors.

During the early days of the Pentecostal Movement in our country, personal character weaknesses and abuse of the gifts of the Holy Spirit on the part of some Pentecostals caused many people to reject the experience of the Baptism in the Holy Spirit.

For example, there were individuals belonging to the denomination in which I grew up who were deceived into making an idol of speaking in tongues. In my generation, although we talked about the Holy Spirit and speaking in tongues, the average churchgoer had no concept of the proper usage and purpose of tongues. The Holy Spirit was regarded as some kind of mystical "force" which mysteriously came upon people, overpowering them with His presence and causing them to do all kinds of weird and unreasonable things. Messages in tongues were given without any interpretation, often at inopportune or inappropriate times, interrupting the service.

Sometimes burning oil or kerosene lamps were taken to individuals in the congregation. An unseen force seemingly caused them to pass their hands through the open flames. The act itself was done to prove that the power of God was present and would prevent damage to the body. God in His mercy protected them through their faith. A few actually believed that this was the power of God moving, but many were repelled by these bizarre actions. In that society, when a person spoke in tongues, he was thought to have achieved the ultimate in spiritual maturity.

Likewise, today there are those who are being deceived concerning intercession. In some circles an "office of intercessor" has been established, in which persons of weak and unstable character and temperament are provided ample opportunity to abuse a God-given privilege. The result is not unity, harmony and peace in the church; it is chaos, disorder and unrest.

In some instances, so-called intercessors have actually alienated the sheep from the shepherd. There are pastors who have lost control of the prayer groups in their churches because they made the mistake of thinking they could safely "leave the praying to others." The culmination of such disruptive activity is often that the pastor demands that the intercessors leave the church. When this happens, a domino effect of hurt and rejection is set off, affecting many church members, as well as the pastor, as he watches his intercessors not only leave but also take many others with them. This ought not to happen. A house divided against itself cannot stand (Matt. 12:25).

Is there an answer? I believe there is. Prayer is a vital pillar in any church or any spiritual endeavor. Without prayer, a church becomes a social organization, failing to meet the spiritual needs of the congregation. Even though the Word of God may be taught, without prayer it becomes a legalistic form, void of power.

Prayer is essential. It is also of utmost importance that intercessors be taught, guided and instructed in the art of intercession—in love and with wisdom. One of Satan's plans for the destruction of the church is to remove effective prayer from the body of Christ, including "divers tongues" and all other spiritual weapons.

My first encounter with familiar spirits was in the early days of leading a prayer group. We unknowingly opened the door for these spirits to mislead us for a short period of time. Our only salvation was our honest hearts and our fervent prayer that God would remove all unfavorable information from our minds so that we would never reveal what had been shown to us.

It was our sincere desire to see those for whom we were interceding freed from demonic oppression. We were relentless in our pursuit of learning how to pray "prayers that avail much." The Holy Spirit, our Teacher, began to show us in John 17 how Jesus interceded for us. Also, He revealed to us that Paul prayed numerous prayers of intercession that we could use as models.

When we do not know how to pray, we have a Helper, the Holy Spirit (Rom. 8:26). Be determined to follow the Spirit of God. Listen to the inner witness and study the Word of God. Trust the Spirit to guide you into all truth by taking the "things" (the ways) of Jesus and revealing them to you, showing you things to come (John 16:13,14).

The anointing of God is on His Word. Praying the Word of God and praying in tongues will break every yoke of bondage. We must be willing to submit to the ministry of the Holy Spirit and not yield to a sense of curiosity and snooping. Valuable time can be wasted on information that the Holy Spirit would never reveal about a person. Since we are not ignorant of the devices of the enemy, let us look at some of the pitfalls designed to stop the "art" of intercession.

Pitfalls of Intercession

Lack of Knowledge

I bear them witness that they have a [certain]
zeal and enthusiasm for God, but it is not
enlightened and according to [correct and
vital] knowledge.

Romans 10:2

The zeal of many Christians far exceeds their ability to rightly interpret the Word of God. Zeal and enthusiasm are necessary in maintaining an effective prayer life, but without revelation knowledge of the Word of God, the intercessor becomes subject to the designs of the devil. God's Word is truth, and when an individual is seeking truth, God will get that truth to him. Jesus said that His sheep know the voice of the Good Shepherd (John 10:3). We cannot know His voice apart from His Word.

In my early days of searching for the truth about how to pray prayers that would avail much, I attended several different prayer groups. I learned more about what *not* to do than what *to* do.

At one church prayer meeting, a young lady, who was a new Christian, wanted the group to pray that a certain mountain of difficulty in her life would be removed and cast into the sea. She went on to reveal that the "mountain" she was referring to was her husband. So dutifully everyone in the group began to pray earnestly that this young woman's husband would be "removed" and "cast into the sea"!

As she gave the account of the problem, it became obvious that the poor man was simply tired of sitting home alone night after night while his wife was out attending prayer meetings, church services, Bible studies and seminars. That night he had asked her to stay home with him, and for that she had informed him that he was of the devil. Understandably, a heated discussion then ensued in the home.

Much zeal in praying about the "removal" of her "problem" was displayed in the prayer session, but a lack of revelation was evident. This young wife needed the wisdom of older women. The leader of the group was responsible for instructing her and the intercessors in revelation knowledge and the proper manner in which to pray for this situation. The pastor of the church was not present, and I don't know if he knew how this prayer meeting was being conducted.

Intercession is a serious business. It can either be a vital asset to a church or a detriment to the spiritual condition and reputation of that ministry. Christians need to adhere to Paul's admonition in 1 Thessalonians

5:12 AMP: *Get to know those who labor among you—recognize them for what they are....*

Those who desire to be in a prayer group should be students of the Word of God and willing to submit to the leader who relies on the written Word for guidance and confirmation. This leader should be properly submitted to the pastor, to those in authority over him or her and to the church doctrines, before attempting to teach revelation knowledge of the Scriptures concerning how to pray effectively.

Misuse of Scriptures

In most prayer groups, the prayer of agreement, as presented by Jesus in Matthew 18:19 KJV, is one of the most misunderstood and abused concepts in the Bible:

Again I say unto you, That if two of you shall agree on earth as touching any thing that they shall ask, it shall be done for them of my Father which is in heaven.

The Lord taught me much about this Scripture after a vivid experience in my marriage. The intercessors in the prayer group, which I had organized, agreed with me that my husband, Everette, would go with me to an upcoming seminar I wanted us to attend together.

At this time Everette did not seem to be interested in the work God had called me to do. (I was seeking more and more of Jesus and would go with friends or alone to hear various Bible teachers.) Although he refused to go with me, Everette did not hinder me from going. After a while my desire to have my husband attend these meetings with me became a consuming fire within me. Many times when alone, I cried all the way to a service because I wanted my life's partner by my side. I tried everything! I would hear testimonies of how God was bringing couples into total harmony and agreement. I even saw it happening in the marriages of some of the ladies who were attending the Bible study that I was teaching.

Everette ignored all my pleas and the devices to which I resorted in my efforts to get him to go with me. At last, I made my request to the group for prayer for my situation. I was sure that my "time" had arrived because the intercessors entered into that prayer of agreement with me. There was no doubt in my mind that Everette would go. I believed the Bible! Hadn't Jesus said that "anything" that we ask in agreement would be done for us of the Father?

The first night of the meeting came and went. But Everette did not. He stayed at home, and I attended with friends. The second night came and went. Everette did not budge. I attended with friends. Finally, it was the third night of the meeting—God's last chance to answer our "binding" prayer of agreement. Two seats were reserved in the front row of the auditorium—one for me, and one for my husband. As the time for the service approached, I turned down all offers of a ride to the meeting because I just *knew* that my night of triumph had arrived.

It was past time to leave for the meeting and I was still waiting, sure that Everette was going. Finally, he turned to me and said, "If you are going to the service tonight, you'd better leave. You're already late."

I struggled to open my mouth in protest that he just *had* to go with me, but before I could form the words, he closed the subject: "You need to know that you and your friends cannot 'confess' me into going. My mind is made up; I am staying home to watch the World Series on television."

At the meeting I was met by an usher who walked me down that long aisle to the reserved seats while everyone's eyes followed me step by step. I knew that God could not fail, so I was convinced that we must have missed God somewhere. Still, I couldn't understand where we had gone wrong. The intercessors and I had done everything we knew how to do, and on top of that, we believed. Besides, hadn't I put "corresponding action" to my faith by refusing all other rides to the meeting? I had acted in accordance with my faith, and that was *supposed* to be the measure of what I received.

There was no lack of zeal on *my* part—or that of the intercessors. But there was also no Everette at the meeting. I sought God, asking for His wisdom and knowledge.

Yes, my friends and I had zeal. However, our zeal for God was not enlightened according to correct and vital knowledge. Without that knowledge, our zeal was worthless. Because of a lack of revelation knowledge, we had misused the prayer of agreement. I had taken Scripture out of context, "confessed" my own selfish desire and then expected God to act in response to my misguided "faith." He didn't do it. God does not violate His Word in order to answer an improper prayer.

When you are searching for truth, the spirit of error cannot prevail for long. God is patient with His people and gives the Holy Spirit to us to instruct us. In this instance, the Spirit began to do His work of enlightenment in me. One word kept coming to my mind, a word I was increasingly sure was God's answer to my question of where we had gone wrong.

The Spirit showed me that in this case what the intercessors and I had engaged in was not spiritual intercession, but *manipulation.* Our "spiritual prayer of agreement" had actually been nothing more than an act of the flesh—one which Paul refers to in Galatians 5:20 KJV as "witchcraft"! We had tried to control another person's actions by use of the intellect through prayer and positive confession. I realized that it was not my friends' agreement that I had needed in that situation—it was Everette's!

That night I released my husband's "freedom of choice" to God. I too was set free. I realized that my husband was not against me, but for me. I returned to him what he had given me—the freedom to hear from God and to obey the voice of the Good Shepherd *as an individual.* The very next year another seminar was scheduled, and to my surprise Everette not only attended voluntarily, he also served as an usher by his own volition. I went with him to all the evening services.

All prayer must be based on Scripture. If you are praying for your mate, pray according to God's Word, not according to your plans, which are often selfish and for your own benefit. You should learn how to love unconditionally and accept your spouse just as God accepted you.

My desire and prayer for Everette became: "Our Father which art in heaven, hallowed be Thy name. Thy kingdom come. Thy will be done in Everette's life, as it is in heaven." The Holy Spirit gave me many other Scriptures of support for this prayer.[1] God forgave me for attempting to usurp my husband's authority and free will.

The only person who never makes a mistake is the one who never does anything. Thank God that *every Scripture is God-breathed (given by His inspiration) and profitable for instruction, for reproof and conviction of sin, for correction of error and discipline in obedience, [and] for training in righteousness (in holy living, in conformity to God's will in thought, purpose and action)* (2 Tim. 3:16). When you make a mistake, ask for forgiveness and receive it. Thank God for the forgiveness and correction so that you will become a fit vessel for the Master's use.

It is imperative that an intercessor heed sound teaching and *be filled with the full (deep and clear) knowledge of His will in all spiritual wisdom [in comprehensive insight into the ways and purposes of God] and in understanding and discernment of spiritual things* (Col. 1:9). The intercessor must remain teachable—as the Amplified Bible says, *Let our lives lovingly express truth [in all things speaking truly, dealing truly, living truly]. Let us grow up in every way* (Eph. 4:15). Do not neglect your study of God's Word. The Holy Spirit will guide you into *all* truth.

Emotion Versus Spirit

Usually there is at least one member in a prayer group who is more emotional than others. For some unknown reason, people will tend to look upon this one as being very spiritual. They will begin to depend on the emotional reactions of this individual as a sign of the effectiveness of their prayers, or for evidence to determine whether the prayer has been answered or not.

For example, if he or she is crying, that is taken as a sign that more intercession is needed. Laughter might mean that the prayer has been heard and answered.

God does not lead us by our emotions, but by His Spirit: *for as many as are led by the Spirit of God, they are the sons of God* (Rom. 8:14 KJV). His Word is a light unto our path and a lamp unto our feet (Ps. 119:105). He leads us by His Word, His peace and the inner witness: *Let the peace (soul harmony which comes) from Christ rule (act as umpire continually) in your hearts—deciding and settling with finality all questions that arise in your minds, in that peaceful state* (Col. 3:15).

The writer of Hebrews asks, *Shall we not much rather be in subjection unto the Father of spirits, and live?* (Heb. 12:9 KJV). God is a spirit, and those who worship Him must do so in spirit and in truth (John 4:24). In Romans 8:14 Paul gives us insight into how we are to relate to God our Father when he points out that those who are led by the Spirit are the true sons of God. Also, Romans 8:16 tells us that the Spirit Himself bears witness with our spirit that we are the children of God.

So, it appears from these Scriptures that God is the One who deals with us Spirit to spirit.

Visions and Voices

Depending on visions and voices apart from the Word of God is dangerous and will lead to spiritual experiences which are not of God. For example, a certain woman who was being ministered to presented her urgent prayer request concerning two rebellious teenagers who were creating problems in her home.

The group immediately went into loud, thunderous, earnest prayer. The answer to the woman's problems was in the Scriptures, but no one offered any scriptural basis for the prayer to be prayed or gave instructions on how to pray. After a while she fell on the floor and a young lady, who seemed to be the leader of the group, began to have a vision of a beautiful casket dripping with jewels. As she finished relating her vision, which offered no answer to the problem at hand, everyone became very excited about the vision which had been recounted in very religious terms.

Later, I tried to share the Word of God with the lady who had the problem. She told me that she wasn't interested in what the Bible had to say because she already felt better. How sad, when she went home, that she faced the same problems; her situation had not changed at all.

Do not be led astray by voices or visions! God is not "flaky" and He does not want His children acting "flaky." Somehow some people have established the idea that to be spiritual one must act weird. *Prayer is a spiritual business, and effective prayers are governed by spiritual laws.* If we adhere to the status and teachings of the Bible, people will be drawn to us, not driven away from us.

Fleshly Manifestations

A letter I received from an intercessory prayer group leader described how two women in her group were acting. When a prayer request was shared, one of the women would begin to act like a dog, getting down on her hands and knees, clawing and scratching. Her friend would then follow her around, "casting out evil spirits," while this woman clawed her legs, even to the point of drawing blood. This practice was driving people away from the group, and the leader did not know how to deal with the situation. Supposedly, the one who acted like a dog took on all the evil spirits of the individual for whom the group was interceding. As her friend "cast out the evil spirits from her," it was said to bring deliverance to the person being tormented.

The pastor was unaware of what was happening in this group. I advised this leader to go to the pastor immediately and explain to him what was taking place. These activities were of the flesh (physical manifestations contrived mentally), but they were applied as if they were spiritually perceived and derived. Later, I received a good report from this church. God had brought them revelation knowledge on prayer through a responsible, effective seminar on intercession.

May God grant that more and more such revelation knowledge and wisdom be forthcoming in the days ahead!

4

Who Is Called To Pray?

A few years ago, after several strenuous days of ministering and taking care of my husband and four children, I walked out of a difficult meeting. I complained loud and long about what I believed to be the root cause of the problem—my intercessors were obviously not doing their job! Had they been, I reasoned, my teaching and ministry would be going much more smoothly and easily.

When I finally settled down long enough to quit murmuring and complaining, the Lord revealed something to me about prayer. It was during football season, and the Lord used a football game (of all things) to show me how He holds each person responsible for his own personal prayer life.

In the illustration He gave me, I saw that the linemen (the intercessors and those in the ministry of helps) were in position, ready to charge the opposing line and open a path for their backfield to break through. Behind them stood the quarterback (the apostle, prophet, evangelist, pastor or teacher), who was responsible for properly reading the defense and calling the right offensive plays. If anyone on the team was out of position or failed to do his job, his actions would affect all the other team members.

Then the Holy Spirit ministered to me that no matter how well the linemen played their positions, since they neither called the plays nor carried the ball, they were very limited in their ability to win the game. Without the well-prepared, mentally alert, physically able-bodied quarterback (the ball handler), theirs was virtually an impossible task. I also realized that the quarterback could not lead his team to victory without the proper preparation and willingness to accept and follow the instructions of his coach.

Once that analogy became clear to me, it didn't take me more than a few seconds to see that I had been wrong in my attitude and actions. I realized that I needed to repent of having laid the blame for my failure on my "teammates" when the real fault was mine for having neglected my duty to spend time conferring directly with my "Divine Coach" and to carefully follow *His* game plan.

The entire body of Christ, working together in harmony with the Holy Spirit and each other, will produce positive results. Every member of the body has a place in the church. Our foundation should be the Word of God; our standard, the banner of love; our clothing, humility.

It is time that we Christians grow into spiritual maturity concerning prayer. Individually, we are parts of one another—mutually dependent upon one another. Jesus did not single out certain individuals to pray. In Luke 18:1, He indicated to us collectively that we *ought always to pray and not to turn coward (faint, lose heart, and give up)*. Everyone is admonished in 1 Timothy 2:1 to offer petitions, prayers, intercession and thanksgiving on behalf of all people. Jesus said for us to watch and pray so that we will not enter into temptation (Matt. 26:41). That injunction includes everybody!

Successful apostles, prophets, evangelists, pastors and teachers (called by God to fulfill their respective offices) are men and women who maintain an effective prayer life. Ideally, they are surrounded by diverse members of the body who have answered the call to pray.

We study the lives of many successful people in the ministry, but it is Jesus who should be our role model for leadership. It is amazing how often we have read the New Testament, seeing the miraculous public ministry of our Lord, but failing to recognize the key to His success. Jesus was a person of prayer; He spent much time fellowshipping with the Father. He spoke what He heard the Father say, and He did what He saw the Father do. Most of those times of prayer and communion were spent in solitude—apart even from His intimate friends and disciples.

In Luke 11:1 we read where Jesus' disciples came to Him and asked Him to teach them to pray. Obviously they recognized that the source of His power emanated from His Father through prayer. Too often our prayer time is controlled by our needs—usually, our desperate needs. Crises, however, never dictated the prayer life of Jesus. He prayed before His times of public ministry and afterwards. The results were evident.

We ourselves have heard and seen *how God anointed and consecrated Jesus of Nazareth with the [Holy] Spirit and with strength and ability and power; how He went about doing good, and in particular, curing all who were harassed and oppressed by [the power of] the devil, for God was with Him* (Acts 10:38). Yet the amazing thing is, Jesus told His followers: *I assure you, most solemnly I tell you, if any one steadfastly believes in Me, he will himself be able to do the things I do; and he will do even greater things than these, because I go to the Father* (John 14:12). Then why are we not yet regularly and systematically producing these "greater works"? Could the answer be a failure to pray? If so, we are not alone in this fault.

When Jesus prayed, the heavens were opened and the will of God was revealed in every situation as the natural was changed into the supernatural and the Father was glorified. In His hour of greatest need, however, Jesus called three of His closest disciples to accompany Him, requesting that they stay awake and pray. They failed Him—just as we often do.

I know today that to accomplish the work of the Lord we need the prayerful aid and support of others. The cooperation of both leadership and laymen is required. The key to purposeful and powerful ministry is prayer—praying prayers that avail much.

Do intercessory prayer groups have a place in the church? I believe that they do and that they can be very beneficial in any church in which the pastor is prepared to assume the God-given responsibility of directing the ministry of intercession under the leadership of the Holy Spirit. Today many pastors are personally leading their intercessors in organized prayer rather than appointing someone else to handle it.

It is necessary that a minister maintain close contact with the prayer group by giving (and receiving) counsel. A group that is led by the pastor himself has direct counsel and knowledge of the specific areas of concern in the church. The mistake that has been made by so many ministers is that of depending solely on the intercessor to hear from God for the direction of the ministry. When this happens, the responsibility for church guidance has been shifted from the pastor to the intercessor. This assignment is not done by God, but by humans.

In that case, the intercessor is placed in a position to exercise control over a ministry in a very subtle manner. If that control is allowed to continue, the results can be detrimental to both the ministry and the intercessor. Team members should not make decisions apart from the leadership. If an intercessor accepts the responsibility of hearing from God for a church or other ministry—whether that responsibility is self-imposed or delegated by the pastor—a door is opened for pride to enter the heart of the intercessor.

The Amplified Bible defines pride as *the spirit that makes one overestimate himself and underestimate others* (Prov. 6:17). There is an established line of authority in the church, and when it is violated, Satan (who is a shrewd legalist) takes advantage of the situation. Many people desire a position of authority in their church or ministry, but few are prepared or equipped to handle the heavy burden of responsibility that goes with authority. No pastor should relinquish entirely to others his God-given privilege and responsibility of spiritual leadership and determination of God's direction for the church.

Neither should a prayer group attempt to assume the responsibility of the pastor, as happened in a certain local church. In that instance, the intercessors took it upon themselves to hear from God for their pastor. The group began receiving "words" about other members of the church. Forgetting that we are not engaged in warfare against flesh and blood, these people began demanding that the pastor turn certain persons out of the church. These intercessors were good people who loved the Lord and truly wanted to work for Him. But when the pastor wisely refused to comply with their demands, rather than being spiritually mature and allowing God to handle the situation, they became self-righteous in their attitude and actions.

The affair concluded with the intercessors leaving the church, still convinced that they were right. They sincerely believed that since they had "heard from God" in the matter, the pastor was obviously in disobedience to God's will and purpose. They failed to see that they had become dictatorial and overbearing. They had unconsciously become guilty of pride—overestimating themselves and underestimating others (namely, their pastor and other members of the congregation).

These ladies were in the infancy stage of prayer and were taking their first steps, and as they grew in knowledge and wisdom, they became productive members in the body of Christ. They believed they were operating in the "discerning of spirits." There is such a thing as the gift of the discerning of spirits. It is referred to in 1 Corinthians 12. But this "gift" operates as the Spirit of God wills; it never becomes the personal "possession" or prerogative of the individual through whom it operates. The deception had given way to a critical and judgmental spirit.

In his book *Questions and Answers on Spiritual Gifts*, Howard Carter points out:

> "There are those who have, perhaps uncon-sciously, criticized their brethren, and have believed they were manifesting this gift [the discerning of spirits] when they supposedly detected 'demon power' in nearly every meeting they have entered. They profess to see demon power in the services, demon influences moving the speaker, demon spirits everywhere. They have accounted for every lack of blessing by demon power only, and they have seen nothing by their supposed exercise of the gift but what has been bad."[1]

If your prayer group is only discerning devils, it is time to seek help. You need to find someone who can train your members in the art of intercession. Intercessory prayer must adhere to Scripture. Constantly looking for problems and inadequacies in every situation leads to operating in negativism instead of in the power of the Holy Spirit. It may be ego-building to suppose that you know the faults of others through the discerning of spirits, but the intercessor must be continually clothed in humility.

The purpose of the gift of the discerning of spirits is "to recognize the presence of Satan in an individual's life to deliver him from Satan's grasp and to glorify Christ. The gift of discerning of spirits also includes the discerning of angelic spirits. God has made angels ministering spirits; many times people discern that an angel is near."[2]

The time has come for the entire church to answer the call to prayer—those in the fivefold ministry and church members alike. We do not need any more divisions, but instead, harmony and agreement, which will only come about if we pray scripturally as led by the Spirit.

In the church at Philippi, there was an occasion for a church to split because two women in positions of leadership were of differing opinions. Paul instructed the church to *help these [two women to keep on cooperating]* (Phil. 4:3), pointing out that they had toiled along with him in the spreading of the Gospel. We can see the attitude in which Paul prayed, and how he prayed, by examining Philippians 1:4: *In every prayer of mine I always make my entreaty and petition for you all with joy (delight).*

As you continue to read the book of Philippians, you will see prayers that Paul prayed for the members while under the inspiration of the Holy Spirit. Here we have an example set before us by one who said, "Follow me as I follow Jesus" (1 Cor. 11:1). Paul, the apostle, prayed for the churches!

We also find in Ephesians 6 that Paul admonished the church at Ephesus to pray. He wrote:

Pray at all times (on every occasion, in every season) in the Spirit, with all [manner of] prayer and entreaty. To that end keep alert and watch with strong purpose and persever-ance, interceding in behalf of all the saints (God's consecrated people). And [pray] also for me, that [freedom of] utterance may be given me, that I may open my mouth to proclaim boldly the mystery of the good news (the Gospel), for which I am an ambassador in a coupling chain [in prison. Pray] that I may declare it boldly and courageously, as I ought to do.

Ephesians 6:18-20

The body of Christ is called to a life of prayer.

Each of us is responsible to adjust our opinions and make a decision to come into the unity of the Spirit and faith by praying according to the Word of God in the Spirit. In Matthew 21:13 Jesus noted, *The Scripture says, My house shall be called a house of prayer.*

Individually, each of us is a temple of the Holy Spirit, or a house of prayer. The many individuals, or houses, make up one great household of prayer. Paul sets forth this concept beautifully in Ephesians 2:20-22.

You are built upon the foundation of the apostles and prophets with Christ Jesus Himself the chief Cornerstone. In Him the whole structure is joined (bound, welded) together harmoniously, and it continues to rise (grow, increase) into a holy temple in the Lord [a sanctuary dedicated, consecrated, and sacred to the presence of the Lord]. In Him [and in fellowship with one another] you yourselves also are being built up [into this structure] with the rest, to form a fixed abode (dwelling place) of God in (by, through) the Spirit.

When each one of us assumes his or her position on the team or in the army of intercessors, miracles will begin to take place, the plan of God for today will start to unfold, and we will become one in Christ Jesus so that the world will know that God the Father has sent His Son for their salvation.

For because of Him the whole body (the church, in all its various parts) closely joined and firmly knit together by the joints and ligaments with which it is supplied, when each part [with power adapted to its need] is working properly [in all its functions], grows to full maturity, building itself up in love.

Ephesians 4:16

As we become more enlightened we are assuming our God-appointed task in prayer, giving place to and esteeming our supporting team members.

5

Guidelines for Intercession

A principle is found in 2 Corinthians 10:13-16 for drawing lines of Christian responsibility. In his writings, the apostle Paul indicates that he will keep within the limits of his commission that God has allotted to him for his measuring line. By this we see that it is not the job of the intercessor to cross lines of scriptural authority by seeking God for direction concerning the operation of another person's ministry.

As an intercessor for a ministry, it is your responsibility to pray for the one who must give an account to God for all ministry decisions. Pray according to the Word of God that the person for whom you are interceding will hear the voice of the Good Shepherd and that he will not follow the voice of a stranger. Directions for the ministry should not be predetermined by the intercessor before the praying begins. Remember, it is to his own Master that the minister will stand or fall, and his Master is able to make him stand (Rom. 14:4). Also, remember to pray for specific situations, such as prayer requests and for meetings, so that the needs of the people who receive ministry will be met.

If the voice which you hear when you are praying is regularly at odds with the voice of the group leader or minister, you need to find out where the problem lies. Is it that you do not believe in the vision and cannot conscientiously support it, or is the problem caused by the fact that the real motive behind your intercession is a selfish one? Intercessors who feel uncomfortable in situations where they are not "in the driver's seat" must allow the Holy Spirit to expose the hidden reasons for their discomfort.

If you are one of those persons, ask yourself these questions: Am I looking for personal power and position? Are titles (such as "Intercessor" or "Coordinator of Intercessory Prayer") important to my sense of self-esteem? Am I truly seeking the welfare and benefit of others, or am I really looking for acceptance and recognition for myself?

It is time to speak truly, deal truly and live truly. Light will dispel the darkness. If a person who is seeking power, position or recognition refuses to allow the Word of God to expose, analyze and judge the very thoughts and purpose of his heart, he will find himself operating in manipulation and witchcraft. He will attempt to impose his personal desires upon a ministry or a church, thus usurping the established, God-instituted authority, if possible.

If there is disagreement and disharmony between the spiritual leader and the intercessor, someone has to yield. If agreement cannot be reached, it may be an indication that the person disagreeing with the vision is out of place. From my own experience, I have found that such is often the case. However, it has been evident to me that people who are out of harmony with their spiritual leader and his God-given vision never really find their niche until they allow the Holy Spirit to create within them a steadfast heart. They must be freed of all jealousy and fear by submitting themselves to another person's ministry.

The most dangerous type of intercessor is the individual who must be in control. Persons of this spirit go from church to church, or group to group, believing that they are there to help guide the pastor into the truth. They feel they are sent by God to keep the pastor straight, to correct his theology and to rearrange his vision. When these persons are asked to step down from their positions, or when they are corrected in some matter, they experience pain and rejection. They still believe that they are right and that everyone else is wrong. They don't realize that by failing (or refusing!) to submit to those in authority, they have brought that pain and rejection upon themselves.

A pastor cannot afford to compromise his vision or to avoid confrontation. Conflicts must be resolved. If problems are not dealt with promptly and decisively, many of God's people will be harmed. If you are called to pray for a ministry, get into agreement with the vision of that ministry and undergird its leader with love, prayer and faith.

Guidelines for the Pastor

Since most intercessory prayer problems arise in the local church, let's consider the relationship of the pastor to the prayer group. It is the duty of the pastor to pray and receive direction for the church body and the different church services for which he is responsible. He is the under-shepherd. As such, he is to lead his people according to the pattern laid down in the Word of God for all pastors:

> *Not by coercion or constraint, but willingly; not dishonorably motivated by the advantages and profits [belonging to the office] but eagerly and cheerfully; not domineering [as arrogant, dictatorial and overbearing persons] over those in your charge, but being*

examples (patterns and models of Christian living) to the flock (the congregation).

1 Peter 5:2,3

My heart is tender toward young pastors who are learning to lead their congregation. I believe that God has given me some guidelines that will help them avoid some mistakes that could delay their progress.

In regard to the intercessory prayer group, the responsibilities of the pastor are to:

1. Be knowledgeable of intercession by precept and practice in order to direct your congregation in praying all manner of prayers.

2. Follow the revealed plan of God. After receiving direction from the Chief Shepherd through personal prayer, effectively communicate that plan to your intercessors.

3. Maintain open communication with the prayer leader.

4. Exercise your responsibility of choosing a prayer leader who is willing to submit to your leadership and to adhere to the church vision: *Now also we beseech you, brethren, get to know those who labor among you* (1 Thess. 5:12).

5. Be careful never to delegate to the prayer group your personal duty and responsibility of praying for the church. As the pastor it is imperative that you maintain your God-given leadership role; the prayer group must follow your example, not the other way around.

6. Be willing to listen to the prayer group leader, remembering that you are not looking for a "yes-man," but for a "check and balance" person. When there is a legitimate difference of opinion concerning the proper direction of the ministry, you will have to determine whether or not to proceed with the proposed plan. You cannot always wait for everyone involved to see things exactly as you see them. However, continue to keep open communication between yourself and your intercessors. Pray according to Philippians 3:15: *So let those [of us] who are spiritually mature and full-grown have this mind and hold these convictions; and if in any respect you have a different attitude of mind, God will make that clear to you also.* We can hold different opinions without disagreement and disharmony, if we respect one another. Our goal should be to have the same opinion.

7. Be willing to admit your own mistakes and correct them, asking for forgiveness when necessary, while maintaining your proper position as under-shepherd of the flock. As a pastor, remain spiritually and mentally alert, and live a life of self-control so you do not bring a reproach to the Gospel.

Your public ministry is a direct result of your prayer life. Jesus' prayer life was His key to success; He prayed and the heavens were opened. However, even He desired and sought prayer support, as evidenced by the fact that He asked His disciples to watch and pray with Him during His time of testing in the Garden of Gethsemane. If the Lord Jesus needed prayer support in His trials, then it seems obvious that those of us in the ministry today must develop and rely on the kind of prayerful aid and support which only other concerned believers can provide.

Guidelines for the Intercessory Prayer Leader

An intercessory prayer leader—one who is assigned by the pastor to look after the business and duty of prayer on behalf of the church and to support its God-given vision—must be of good and attested character and repute, full of the Spirit and wisdom of God (Acts 6:3).

The leader should be spiritually sensitive to unity within the prayer group. If you see that there are those in the group who are having difficulty praying in a particular area, do not pursue that directive for prayer. How can two walk together except they be in agreement? (Amos 3:3).

It is when we are united in prayer that the power of God is released. It is not the responsibility of the group to pray contrary to the desires of its own members for the decisions of the church leadership. However, all matters of difficulty or disagreement need to be reported to those in authority so they can be resolved.

The prayer group leader must be mature enough to be willing to wait before God and remain teachable. In a multitude of counselors there is safety (Prov. 24:6). A God-given leader is one who has learned to recognize and obey spiritual authority.

The duties of the responsible intercessory prayer leader are to:

1. Stay in close contact with the pastor in order to promote harmony, and keep prayer within the parameters of the church vision and the Word of God. At the discretion of the pastor, prayer

coordinators may attend church staff meetings and come into the church office for private consultations when needed.

2. Maintain order in the group by setting guidelines according to scriptural principles.

3. Unite the people in the group by setting forth specific areas for prayer.

4. Nurture group members by helping them to develop Christian character while being knit together in love.

5. Make and keep members aware that they are a part of a much larger body. The leader must discourage and avoid the development of a clique or secret society. Keep the door open for new members (intercessors) to join the group.

6. Pray for the needs of group members outside the group prayer time.

7. Be ready to teach on intercession when needed.

Guidelines for a Group Member

A member of an intercessory prayer group must be teachable, willing to yield to reason, a student of God's Word, a worshiper of the true God and respectful of his assigned leader. If a true intercessor has difficulty with a direction offered by the leader, then it is advisable for the leader to listen, just as it is advisable for the pastor to listen to his intercessors. However, the final decision must remain with the one in charge.

When that person's decision is to overrule the objection and to proceed as he sees fit, the intercessor meets his first soul-searching test of commitment. He should ask himself: "Has God really called me to pray for this man and this church? If so, am I willing to submit to this established leadership? If I am not willing to submit, is it because I am seeking position or power for myself instead of God's blessing for others?" Many times, these questions are not easily answered.

A group member must recognize and remember that the group leader is acting in the place of the pastor and represents an important link in the chain of command set in the church. The motto or slogan of each prayer group member should be the admonishment given all believers in the book of Hebrews: *Obey your spiritual leaders and submit to them* (Heb. 13:17).

Your responsibilities as a group member are to:

1. Lay down your life for the congregation by setting aside the fulfillment of your own personal desires and needs for the sake of others. It is your responsibility to pray for your own family in private. Generally, group intercessory prayer

time is on behalf of specific prayer for others; therefore, personal prayer requests by individual group members should not be submitted at this time.

2. Be confident and unwavering in your commitment to God, your pastor, your group leader and to the particular church body for which the group is praying.

3. Prepare your heart for prayer ahead of time. Loose yourself from wrong attitudes—resentment, unforgiveness, criticism and judgmentalism (Matt. 6:12; 7:1). Yield the members of your body as instruments of righteousness unto God.

4. Submit to the leadership and follow the flow of the group spirit under the direction of the leader. No individual member should insist on having his own way (1 Cor. 13:4-8).

5. Share, at the appropriate time, what the Holy Spirit has ministered to you personally in given areas of prayer.

6. Be careful not to neglect other areas of ministry in the church. Be a doer of the Word and the work of God (James 1:22,25).

7. Spend time with God in praise and worship apart from the group prayer time.

8. Place a guard over your mouth. Do not boast about the things God is revealing during intercession. The true intercessor is not seeking position, reputation or attention, but is always looking for ways to glorify and serve God the Father (2 Cor. 10:17).

Over the years, I have attended many prayer groups. Each one had its own personality. I have seen positive results produced by all different types of prayer activity. We have to ask ourselves how this can be. The only possible answer is that the heart motives of the group are more important to God than outward form or prescribed procedure. We know that God's Word does not return to Him void of power and purpose. When God's people come together with pure hearts, unselfish motives and faith in Him, believing that He will perform His Word, then their intercessory efforts produce prayers that avail much (James 5:16).

Some people enter into prayer with an almost incredible viciousness. They almost seem to reach down, pick up the devil, wrap their arms around his shoulders and demand a wrestling match with him. They scream, yell, throw karate chops and launch themselves both physically and emotionally into the fight against what appear to be flying rebel spirits.

There are other groups who pray according to a set pattern, joining their voices together in united prayer. They follow written scriptural prayers, lifting their hearts as one before the Father.

Others pray "together" simply and unpretentiously, but without any set form or order. Quietly and unemotionally, they lift their hearts and voices simultaneously by praying individually in the Spirit.

In some instances, the group leader announces the topics for prayer with applicable Scriptures as a point of reference. The group members then pray in accordance with the leader as the Holy Spirit leads from one subject to another. Others write all prayer requests on a board, and as people file in to the meeting, they select subjects for which they feel led to pray.

Some groups pray loudly, some quietly, some even silently. There are some whose primary weapon of warfare is praise and worship. Others begin to moan and groan, preparing for travail.

There are some groups that place great emphasis on physical activities, such as barking like dogs, lying on top of others to impart anointing to them or staring at pictures or paintings until mesmerized. In my opinion, such activity repels decency and order. In such groups, membership usually becomes selective; only the "elect" or the "elite" of the church can be admitted. This itself is a warning sign.

I have found that prayer groups that function entirely without a leader soon dissolve. This is also true of groups in which everything is "spiritualized" to the point of ignoring practical obligations, such as going to work, the preparation of meals and the care of families or homes.

The main problem with prayer group intercession arises when individual groups begin to believe that the way they conduct their prayer service is the (one and only) "correct" manner and that everyone else is wrong. This attitude has been a tool of the enemy bringing intimidation, distrust and disharmony into the church with the intention of stopping real heartfelt fervent prayer on behalf of the saints.

My position is this: let each prayer group develop according to the pattern which it believes God has given it. Follow after the Spirit, who will never cause us to violate the Word of God. Remain teachable and be willing to conform your own personal or group opinions to the Word of God.

I believe there are scriptural instructions on how to enter into prayer—both privately and corporately. A person must know where he is in relation to his commander and his enemy. Likewise, we first need to locate Jesus, ourselves and the enemy.

Today, *Jesus* is physically removed from the surface of the earth. The apostle Paul tells us:

He [God] *raised Him* [Jesus] *from the dead and seated Him at His [own] right hand in the heavenly [places], far above all rule and authority and power and dominion and every name that is named [above every title that can be conferred], not only in this age and in this world, but also in the age and the world which are to come. And He has put all things under His feet and has appointed Him the universal and supreme Head of the church [a headship exercised throughout the church], which is His body, the fullness of Him Who fills all in all [for in that body lives the full measure of Him Who makes everything complete, and Who fills everything every-where with Himself].*

Ephesians 1:20-23

Physically, *you and I* are here on earth, but spiritually we are positioned in heaven, because *He* [God] *raised us up together with Him* [Christ] *and made us sit down together [giving us joint seating with Him] in the heavenly sphere* (Eph. 2:6). Where? *Far above all rule and authority and power and dominion and every name that is named [above every title that can be conferred], not only in this age and in this world, but also in the age and the world which are to come* (Eph. 1:21).

Some time ago, the Lord graciously gave me a dream which illustrates the location of the *enemy*. In my dream, I walked into my gleaming white kitchen and saw what appeared to be an army of common house roaches advancing toward me. Naturally, I was repelled and began to draw back. Immediately, I became aware that these were no ordinary roaches but vile little creatures with different-colored bodies which flashed like neon lights. Spontaneously, a strength began to surge up from within me and I thought, *Why, I shouldn't be shrinking back from these ugly little insects; I can step on each one of them and destroy them.* With newfound courage, I changed my tactic from retreat to attack. As I advanced toward the loathsome little beasts, they began to run from me. Just then, I woke up.

Immediately upon my awakening, the Holy Spirit reminded me of the words spoken by our Lord Jesus Christ, as recorded in Luke 10:19 KJV: *Behold, I give unto you power to tread on serpents and scorpions, and over all the power of the enemy: and nothing shall by any means hurt you.*

According to Ephesians 1, Satan is underneath our feet, because all things have been subordinated to (put under the feet of) Jesus. That means that since we are the body of Christ here on this earth, Satan and his kingdom of darkness are under *our* feet. The church of Jesus Christ has been given authority and power over Satan and his demons. Our enemy is involuntarily in subjection to the church.

Jesus has won the victory. He is the Captain of this great army of saints. He has spoiled the principalities of darkness, making a show of them openly, triumphing over them (Col. 2:15).

God has not called you and me to a worrisome, irksome task. He has called us to a life of powerful communion with Him in which we will experience victory and "joy unspeakable" (1 Peter 1:8).

Christian, rise up and take your place in this glorious life of intercessory prayer!

6

How To Enter In

It has been noted that intercessors sometimes become heavy ladened, overburdened and oppressed. There are those who think that this is the inevitable condition of the true intercessor. Their countenance is sad and they carry their prayer loads for the entire world to see.

In Philippians 1:4, the apostle Paul writes, *In every prayer of mine I always make my entreaty and petition for you all with joy (delight).* Intercessors, do not become so overwhelmed by the needs of others that you neglect intimate fellowship with God. Determine that you will be in true communion with your Father each and every day.

Moses was an intercessor who knew how to enter into this communication with God. The Lord promised that His presence would go with Moses and that He would give him rest. Moses knew that the key to experiencing this rest was spending time alone with God. In order for you to prepare for intercession, you will find it necessary to do as Moses did. Make time every day for communion with your Father—spirit to Spirit.

Psalm 100 gives an outline for entering into the presence of God, which is where true intercession should begin:

First, *Make a joyful noise to the Lord* (v. 1). Do this regardless of circumstances! Say, "This is the day which the Lord has made; I will rejoice and be glad in it" (Ps. 118:24).

Second, *Serve the Lord with gladness! Come before His presence with singing!* (Ps. 100:2). Begin your time of intercession by delighting yourself in the Lord, for happy is the person whose God is the Lord (Ps. 144:15). He requires that those who are His serve Him with gladness of heart. He has supplied fountains of joy within us—He has made us glad! (Ps. 92:4.) Come into His presence with singing for He has put a new song in our heart. Release it in words and music, *Speak out...in psalms and hymns and spiritual songs, ...making melody with all your heart to the Lord* (Eph. 5:19). Dance before Him, putting off burdens and heavy loads. Make a joyful noise to the Lord!

Third, *Know (perceive, recognize, and understand with approval) that the Lord is God! It is He Who has made us, not we ourselves [and we are His]! We are His people and the sheep of His pasture* (Ps. 100:3).

Exalt the Lord your God (Ps. 99:5). The Word is God, and in order to know Him, you must become acquainted with Him through His Word (the Bible) and the Holy Spirit (our Teacher).

Today, so often the work of the enemy is attributed to God by people who have not taken the time to get acquainted with "our Father which art in heaven." They are unable to "hallow" His name because they do not know His character.

In order to pray effectively, we must know our God. The many different names of God reveal His nature and character.[1] We do not dictate our will to God, but rather we remember that He is the Maker, the Creator and the Potter. We are His people and the sheep of His pasture.

Do you know the kind of person you are? Through the positive confession of God's Word, you can begin to see yourself as God sees you. Sometimes it is our mind that is our own worst enemy. We become deceived in areas in which we merely listen to the Word of God but never obey it. The Word must be applied to our daily living. We must believe what God says about us in His Word.

It is imperative, for instance, that you know who you are—God's handiwork, recreated in Christ Jesus, His very own workmanship. As you pray, you will begin to see yourself and others as God sees His people—the sheep of His pasture. This perspective will build your confidence toward God and your faith in the ability which God has placed within you to pray effectively.

This, then, is the third step to entering into intercessory prayer—to declare who God is and who He created you to be.

Fourth, *Enter into His gates with thanksgiving and a thank offering and into His courts with praise! Be thankful and say so to Him, bless and affectionately praise His name!* (Ps. 100:4.) Be grateful to the Lord for what He has done and for the things that He has given you. Do not come to the place where you take God and His works for granted. Reiterate His wondrous works and mighty deeds in your life and in the lives of those for whom you intercede. You are responsible for praying for the members of your family. God is looking for an intercessor in each family who will love as Jesus loves, laying down his (or her) life for family members and loved ones.

My mother, Donnis Brock Griffin, was the first one in her family to receive Jesus as her Lord and Savior. As a fifteen-year-old, she paved the way for her entire family (including her parents) to come to the knowledge of the truth. Later she and my dad were married. As we children were born, my mother began to pray diligently for us. Until she went to be with the Lord at the age of eighty-one, her daily prayers included not only her children, but their spouses, her grandchildren and great-grandchildren. Today, her prayer mantle has passed down to others. She declared on the authority of God's Word that all of her posterity belongs to the kingdom of God.

Since you have answered the call to pray, assume the responsibility of praying for your family. When praying as part of a group, leave requests for family situations for your personal prayer times.

In Philippians 4:6, Paul urges, *Do not fret or have any anxiety about anything, but in every circumstance and in everything, by prayer and petition (definite requests), with thanksgiving, continue to make your wants known to God.*

Fifth, *For the Lord is good; His mercy and loving-kindness are everlasting, His faithfulness and truth endure to all generations* (Ps. 100:5). Remember this truth and rejoice in it.

The intercessor is not to be of a sad countenance, burdened or heavy laden. Happy are we whose God is the Lord. Most intercessors I know have a good sense of humor, and they are quick to laugh. Should you feel overburdened, run to Jesus who said:

Come to Me, all you who labor and are heavy-laden and overburdened, and I will cause you to rest. [I will ease and relieve and refresh your souls.]

For My yoke is wholesome (useful, good—not harsh, hard, sharp, or pressing, but comfortable, gracious, and pleasant), and My burden is light and easy to be borne.

Matthew 11:28,30

In His presence you are relieved of heavy burdens and set free to become a co-laborer with God. The intercessor should be the most joyous person on earth. *In Your presence* [the Lord's] *is fullness of joy, at Your right hand there are pleasures forevermore* (Ps. 16:11). The Holy Spirit will show you the pathway to a life of prayer.

By entering into a time of praise and worship, using Psalm 100 as a model, each person has the opportunity to lay aside thoughts which interfere with *being in full accord and of one harmonious mind and intention* (Phil. 2:2). You have the mind of Christ and hold the thoughts, feelings and purposes of His heart (1 Cor. 2:16). In His presence it is easy to *let this same attitude and purpose and [humble] mind be in you which was in Christ Jesus* (Phil. 2:5).

His purpose is stated in Luke 4:18-19:

The Spirit of the Lord [is] upon Me, because He has anointed Me [the Anointed One, the Messiah] to preach the good news (the Gospel) to the poor; He has sent Me to announce release to the captives and recovery of sight to the blind, to send forth as delivered those who are oppressed [who are downtrodden, bruised, crushed and broken down by calamity], to proclaim the accepted and acceptable year of the Lord [the day when salvation and the free favors of God profusely abound].

You join with the Lord in His purpose when you pray for the poor, those in captivity, the blind and the oppressed who are downtrodden, bruised, crushed and broken by calamity. Through intercessory prayer, you bring to them salvation and the free favors of God.

Begin to pray for others as the Holy Spirit leads, remembering that He does not lead apart from the Word of God. Learn to hear His voice. Jesus said:

I am the good shepherd, and know my sheep, and am known of mine.

And a stranger will they not follow, but will flee from him: for they know not the voice of strangers.

John 10:14,5 KJV

There are many voices, many languages. Paul says that none of them is without significance (1 Cor. 14:10). Some individuals say that God has never spoken to them, but He has—through the pages of sixty-six books which are bound into two volumes: the Old Testament and the New Testament. God's Word will endure forever.

Know God, know His Word and pray according to His will. Locate your faith, because when you find God's will on a subject, you must mix faith with what you "hear" (the written Word). You must believe to be true that for which you are praying, and pray with conviction.

Never add to God's will by reading into the Scriptures something which they do not say. For instance, you cannot take Psalm 37:4 *(Delight yourself also in the Lord, and He will give you the desires and secret petitions of your heart)* and use it as a basis for asking God for another person's mate or house or car. That would be adding to God's stated will. This manner of praying will produce disastrous results, hurting many people, rather than bringing glory to the Father.

When praying, the motive and intent of the heart must be right before the Lord. In James 4:2-3 the apostle tells his first century readers:

You do not have, because you do not ask.

[Or] you do ask [God for them] and yet fail to receive, because you ask with wrong purpose and evil, selfish motives.

It is imperative that our petitions and intercessions be made out of a heart of selflessness. True intercession is rooted and grounded in *agape* love.

When you are praying God's will for someone, it is not necessary to tell that person about your intercession. Remember, you cannot force anyone to obey God. For example, the husband cannot demand that his wife respect and honor him; neither can the wife demand that her husband love her as Christ loved the church. It is God who watches over His Word to perform it (Jer. 1:12). Your responsibility is to pray. God will assume His responsibility and bring His words to pass as you apply them through your intercession.

The Word of God says, in order to be saved you *must believe in the Lord Jesus Christ [give yourself up to Him, take yourself out of your own keeping and entrust yourself into His keeping] and you will be saved, [and this applies both to] you and your house-hold as well* (Acts 16:31). Pray without adding anything to God's will; believe and walk in love.

One woman shared how she had prayed almost daily for three years for her alcoholic brother to be saved. She added to God's will by telling God how to perform His Word. After becoming very weary, she asked the Lord what else she could do to receive the answer to her prayers. He told her that it was time for her to believe His promises! It was only a short time after she had begun to believe and have faith in God's Word that what she had been asking in prayer came to pass. She saw the salvation of God in that situation.

Your prayers for your family will avail much. Never give up—stand, and having done all, stand (Eph. 6:13).

Never give up on your local church. Jesus said, *Upon this rock I will build my church; and the gates of hell shall not prevail against it* (Matt. 16:18 KJV). A small church in Alabama found itself with only eight members and no pastor. Those eight people discovered God's will for their church, mixed faith with His will and prayed. Two years later, they not only had a pastor, but they outgrew their building. Many financial miracles have occurred and a community, along with its surrounding area, came to know God. When people pray and believe God's Word, He is moved to action on their behalf.

You can be assured that your prayers will avail much when you pray according to God's will, mix faith with your prayers and walk in love.

For as the rain and snow come down from the heavens, and return not there again, but water the earth and make it bring forth and sprout, that it may give seed to the sower and bread to the eater, so shall My word be that goes forth out of My mouth: it shall not return to Me void [without producing any effect, useless], but it shall accomplish that which I please and purpose, and it shall prosper in the thing for which I sent it.

Isaiah 55:10,11

It is my prayer that when Jesus returns, He will find you experiencing the joys of effectual intercessory prayer and will say to you, *Well done, you upright (honorable, admirable) and faithful servant! You have been faithful and trustworthy over a little; I will put you in charge of much. Enter into and share the joy (the delight, the blessedness) which your master enjoys* (Matt. 25:21).

7

Christ and His Church

Many believers become apprehensive at the thought of what is termed "spiritual warfare." Let me assure you that there is nothing to fear. Certain aspects of the true church of Jesus Christ provide us with our confidence in His victory for a glorious world in the kingdom, in the air and in eternity. Initially, we need to know about the foundation of the church and our responsibility in it, and we need to examine various Scriptures which relate to it as the Lord leads us.

"Who Am I?"

When Jesus came into the coasts of Caesarea Philippi, he asked his disciples, saying, Whom do men say that I the Son of man am?

*And they said, Some say that thou art
John the Baptist: some, Elias; and others,
Jeremias, or one of the prophets.*

*He saith unto them, But whom say ye
that I am?*

*And Simon Peter answered and said,
Thou art the Christ, the Son of the living God.*

*And Jesus answered and said unto him,
Blessed art thou, Simon Bar-jona: for flesh
and blood hath not revealed it unto thee, but
my Father which is in heaven.*

*And I say also unto thee, That thou art
Peter* [a fragment of a rock], *and upon this
rock* [an immovable stone, Christ Jesus
Himself] *I will build my church; and the gates
of hell shall not prevail against it.*

Matthew 16:13-18 KJV

Jesus not only promises that He will build the
church, but He also promises that the gates of hell shall
not prevail against it. This tells me that we Christians
are already winners in the face of all opposition to the
Gospel of Christ.

Jesus has already given us authority and power over
all the power of the devil, and we are the enforcers of
His triumphant victory. When He gave His church the
keys to the kingdom, He, in fact, gave us the ability, the
power and the authority to overcome all the strategies

of the enemy. Jesus gave us the keys of the kingdom of heaven—and whatsoever we bind on earth will be bound in heaven; and whatsoever we loose on earth shall be loosed in heaven (Matt. 18:18).

Jesus, the Son of God

First let's ask: Who do we say that Jesus is? Isn't it wonderful that through the revelation knowledge that was given to Peter, and also given to us, we can know that Jesus is the Son of the living God? This Jesus is the Captain of our salvation and He leads us in His triumphant victory over the adversary. The very foundation of our prayer life is based on this question: Who do we say that Jesus is?

Jesus, the Founder of the Church

The second question is: Who is building the church? *Jesus!* He said that He would build His church upon the revelation spoken by Peter—the revelation that "Thou art the Christ, the Son of the Living God." This was a disclosure of Himself, the Rock of Ages.

In Matthew 16:18 Jesus said, "Upon this rock I will build My church." On the Day of Pentecost, Peter spoke forth a proclamation of this revelation, bringing deliverance and salvation to three thousand souls. It was Simon Peter who later called Jesus a "living stone" (1 Peter 2:4 KJV), the "chief corner stone" (v. 6), a "stone of stumbling" and a "rock of offence" (v. 8). Then it was Peter who defined believers as "lively stones." (v. 5.)

The church is built upon the foundation of the apostles and prophets, Jesus Christ Himself being the chief cornerstone (Eph. 2:19-22). We are the church; the church of Jesus Christ is made up of people whom Peter calls "lively stones."

Lively Stones

The term "lively stones" implies that we are in the process of building something as well as being built into a structure, a dwelling place of God. Jesus has assumed His responsibility in building the church. He firmly joins and knits us together as each "stone" works properly in all its functions, growing up to full maturity and building up one another in love (Eph. 4:16).

Now it is time for us to assume our responsibility as members of the household of faith. Through intercession we repair breaches, restore streets to dwell in and build up a highway which leads from Satan's domain to life and peace, reconciliation and salvation—the Kingdom of God (Isa. 58:12; Ez. 22:30). It was Isaiah who cried, *Go through, go through the gates! Prepare the way for the people. Cast up, cast up the highway. Gather out the stones. Lift up a standard or ensign over and for the peoples* (Isa. 62:10).

God Himself is our shield; He is our fortress; and He is our fortification; but we are the lively stones that make up the wall and overthrow the plots of the evil one. Jesus is building His house.

Rebuilding the Wall

We turn to the Old Testament for a look at the rebuilding of Jerusalem, where worship was restored after the return of the Jews from Babylon. In the book of Nehemiah, it was the people who built the wall and God who fought their battle against their enemies. Even though there was great opposition to the building of the wall around Jerusalem, it was completed.

It is interesting that when the Israelites began to build the wall, the enemy became very upset; Sanballat was *wroth, and took great indignation, and mocked the Jews* and Tobiah, the Ammonite, declared that even a fox could break down their wall by simply walking on top of it (Neh. 4:1-3 KJV).

When you and I begin a work for the kingdom of God, the enemy makes it his business to throw obstacles into our paths. However, we are lively stones, strong in the Lord and the power of His might. We are not ignorant concerning the devices of the evil one (2 Cor. 2:11).

Nehemiah tells us:

Those who built the wall and those who bore burdens loaded themselves so that every one worked with one hand and held a weapon with the other hand, and every builder had his sword girded by his side, and so worked. And he who sounded the trumpet was at my side.

Nehemiah 4:17,18

In the New Testament we discover that God through Christ Jesus has fought our battle. Jesus is building His church; we are co-laborers with Him; and the Holy Spirit has been sent to aid and bear us up in our inability to produce results. We do not always know which prayer to offer or how to offer it as worthily as we ought. In our inabilities and weaknesses God's strength is made perfect. That which is impossible with man is possible with God. We believers have no reason to be afraid of the enemy for God is on our side. We stand in readiness for the attacks of the enemy, loaded with the armor of God and our sword, the Word of God (Eph. 6).

The Holy Spirit knows where the enemy is attacking and gives the trumpet sound—our call to pray. Our enemies cannot be seen with the natural eye. You and I are not battling against flesh and blood; we are not praying against people. Our fight is *the good fight of the faith* (1 Tim. 6:12), which takes place in the spiritual realm. We stand against principalities, against powers, against the rulers of the darkness of this world and wicked spirits in heavenly places.

Reconcilers to Truth

As intercessors we are a vital part of life transformations, we are reconcilers to truth. Humbly we receive the word planted in our hearts which sets us free from all our own destructions. We are empowered to lay aside every weight that would hinder us. It is imperative that we live a lifestyle of prayer, "speaking truly, dealing truly and living truly" (Eph. 4:15).

Peter defines the approach to this lifestyle in 1 Peter 2:1 TLB: *So get rid of your feelings of hatred. Don't just pretend to be good! Be done with dishonesty and jealousy and talking about others behind their backs.*

It is our responsibility to guard our hearts and recognize that people are not our problem. One of the most successful strategies of the devil is sowing discord among the believers through the power of thoughtless words often spoken by wounded believers. His objective is to divide and conquer—to set husband against wife and Christian against Christian. Therefore, we have to lay aside all malice, all guile, all hypocrisies, all envies and all evil speaking. We are to hold the thoughts, feelings and purposes of God's heart. God has said that His grace is sufficient for us (2 Cor. 12:9), and it is His grace that enables us to obey the Scriptures.

Speaking, Dealing and Living Truly

Allowing that we have rationalized our intentions and played mind games with ourselves, we must recognize that it takes the work of the Holy Spirit within us to expose malice and ill will toward others. A necessary ingredient in effectual prayer strategy (a truth which I believe cannot be repeated often enough) is that we must always speak truly, deal truly and live truly.

This does not mean pointing the finger at the other person (trying to remove the splinter that is in his eye), but taking moral inventory of ourselves (removing the plank that is in our own eye). We do not wait until we are perfect to pray, but we purpose to have right attitudes and pure hearts. Let us destroy all strongholds.

It is particularly easy for us to involve ourselves in hypocrisies and spiritual pride when we are spiritually immature and emotionally crippled. Hidden hurts and unacknowledged anger are opposing forces that will dominate and control us, causing us to give in to our own systematic rigidity and deception. We must be constantly on guard against dogmatic, judgmental and critical attitudes lest we give place to the devil and our prayers be hindered.

Christian Maturity

Mature Christians should bear the weaknesses of others, keeping their hearts pure, desiring the sincere milk of the Word that they may grow thereby (1 Peter 2:2). It is by the Word of God that we mature, being constantly renewed in the spirit of our mind, that is, having a fresh mental and spiritual attitude which displaces strongholds and man-made defenses that interfere with true intercession (Rom. 12:2).

We are precious in God's kingdom, and it is our responsibility to walk in that which He has provided for us. He has provided us with both relationship and position. Our relationship with God and man is "servant"; our position is "priest" in a holy priesthood.

If so be ye have tasted that the Lord is gracious. To whom coming, as unto a living stone, disallowed indeed of men, but chosen of God, and precious, ye also, as lively stones,

*are built up a spiritual house, an holy priest-
hood, to offer up spiritual sacrifices, acceptable to God by Jesus Christ.*

1 Peter 2:3-5 KJV

Therefore, one of the first principles of intercessory prayer is our recognition that we are a holy priesthood, and we must first give attention to the praise and
worship of our God.

Learn to appropriate the garment of praise to usher
you into the place of victorious intercession. Many
opposing forces are sent to overcome you and destroy
your effectiveness in the kingdom of God. Praise will
stop and impede the avenger who has come to deter
you and cause you to faint, lose heart or give up.
Preparing for intercession through praise enables you to
speak the Word which goes forth like a guided missile
and hits its target.

The Garment of Praise

There was a time when I had grown weary in well-
doing. It seemed that the very life of God was drained
from me. Early one Sunday I was trying to prepare
myself for the morning service when the phone rang. It
was my mom, saying, "Germaine, I received today's
church bulletin in the mail yesterday. Now do what it

says to do—praise!" I promised her that I would pray the prayer of commitment, "To Rejoice in the Lord," from my book, *Prayers That Avail Much, Volume 1*.

Believe me, I did not feel like praying; I did not feel like ministering to anyone; and I certainly did not feel like praising. Very feebly I began to rejoice in the Lord. As I continued, I became stronger and stronger. As I began swinging my arms, shouting and dancing all over my kitchen, the spirit of heaviness left and I was clothed in the garment of praise.

You have to have a made-up mind to praise and worship God. The enemy would like to silence you—to keep you quiet. *From the lips of children and infants you have ordained praise because of your enemies, to silence the foe and the avenger* (Ps. 8:2 NIV).

The word *praise* also means strength, according to the *King James Version*. The psalmist David was not quiet in his praise to his God. Joyous people in the Scriptures were not silent people; they made a joyful noise unto the Rock of their salvation (Ps. 95:1). *O clap your hands, all ye people; shout unto God with the voice of triumph* (Ps. 47:1 KJV). Again and again David admonished the people of his day, *Sing praises to God, sing praises: sing praises unto our King, sing praises* (Ps. 47:6 KJV). In Psalm 34:1 KJV he wrote, *I will bless the Lord at all times: his praise shall continually be in my mouth.*

If you will praise the Lord, the Holy Spirit will give you new songs which you have never heard before. The Holy Spirit, your Teacher, will bring New Testament Scriptures into focus as you speak to yourself *in psalms and hymns and spiritual songs, singing and making melody in your heart to the Lord* (Eph. 5:19 KJV).

Then, out of the abundance of the heart, the mouth speaks (Luke 6:45). If it's in your heart, it will come out your mouth. Release the glad heart and joyous spirit that God has given you. Worshiping in spirit and in truth applies pressure to the rivers of living water that flow out of your innermost being like a mighty life stream.

Don't wait until you feel like it before you begin praising the Lord. Do it because the Bible says to and you will find that you have joined a heavenly host who are praising God in the highest.

Begin your day by proclaiming praises unto your Father: "Father, this is the day that You have made. I will rejoice and be glad in it! The spirit of rejoicing, joy and laughter are my heritage. I will praise You with joyful lips. I am always filled and stimulated by the Holy Spirit. Where Your Spirit is, Lord, there is liberty—emancipation from bondage, freedom. I walk in that liberty.

"I speak out in psalms and hymns and make melody with all my heart to You, Lord. My happy heart is a good medicine and my cheerful mind works healing. Your joy is my strength, Lord. Therefore, I can count it all joy, all strength, when I encounter tests or trials of any sort because I am strong in You, Lord, and in the power of Your might.

"I have the victory in the name of Jesus. Satan is under Jesus' feet. I will not be moved by adverse circumstances."[1]

Most of the time entering into a time of intercessory prayer follows praise and worship to God. (Not always though; we can't be dogmatic about these things.) It is the Holy Spirit who leads us and helps us pray effectively. He knows where the next attack will take place, and He strengthens us when we take our stand against the opposing forces of darkness.

We must get ourselves into a position to hear from the Holy Spirit who is always present. I believe that He is constantly attempting to lead us. The reason we have to spend time in praise and worship is so we can quiet our minds and position ourselves to hear what the Holy Spirit is saying.

A Royal Priesthood

You will note in 1 Peter 2:5 KJV that the writer tells us that we are a "holy priesthood." Then in verse 9 he calls believers a "royal priesthood." Now, not only do we act to fulfill our position as holy priests unto God, but we also accept our role as royal priests. To do that, we must first understand the function of the high priest in the Old Testament and then look at the priest in the role of intercessor.

Once a year the high priest was permitted to go into the holy place of the temple where he met with God. The Lord said of Aaron in Exodus 28:29 KJV, *Aaron shall bear the names of the children of Israel in the breastplate of judgment upon his heart, when he goeth in unto the holy place, for a memorial before the Lord continually.*

The high priest acted as a mediator—an intercessor—on behalf of the people, appearing before God for them. An intercessor is one who prays for others. The priests were the designated intercessors of the Old Testament. Since you and I belong to this priesthood, we are all empowered to pray and intercede for others.

Priests were constantly reminded of their allotted intercession. The names of the tribes of Israel were engraved on precious stones attached to the ephod and the breastplate, which were parts of the priestly robe. The high priest bore the burden of the people upon his shoulders and heart to identify with their need for intercession. Praying on behalf of the people was his perpetual assignment.

What has God placed upon your heart? It is He who assigns, who places "prayer burdens" upon the heart; some remain for a short period of time while others are more persistent.

Intercession on behalf of your government, your family or your church, for instance, is an extended prayer assignment. Sometimes you will find yourself praying regularly for a specific nation or ministry. One lady prays every day for the Jewish people and is acutely interested in reading or viewing anything she finds concerning them. She has already visited the Holy Land and desires to return to Israel. The names of people or their faces may come before you as a prompting from the Holy Spirit, calling you to prayer. At times you will intercede momentarily for someone known or unknown.

Faith Mixed With the Word

One of the quickest ways to sabotage your prayers of petition, supplication and intercession is to become confused about the will of God concerning that for which you are praying. Your faith mixed with God's Word will dispel confusion and insure answered prayer. *Wherefore also it is contained in the scripture, Behold, I lay in Sion a chief corner stone, elect, precious: and he that believeth on him shall not be confounded* (1 Peter 2:6 KJV). To be "confounded" is to be confused, and confusion is an enemy to answered prayer.

As long as our faith is based on truth and our faith is active, we will not become confused. There are many voices out there to distract us. We must know the Word of God and mix our faith with it, knowing that the Father's voice is our surety.

Speaking of the Lord Jesus, Peter tells us:

Unto you therefore which believe he is precious: but unto them which be disobedient, the stone which the builders disallowed, the same is made the head of the corner, and a stone of stumbling, and a rock of offence, even to them which stumble at the word, being disobedient.

1 Peter 2:7,8 KJV

The disobedient are those who stumble over the Word of God.

Other than the Holy Spirit, the most vital aspect involved in our triumphant stand against the enemy is the Word of God. As intercessors, it isn't enough for us just to know the Word. We must be obedient to the Word, not stumbling over it again and again by refusing to obey it. We must live in such a manner that the enemy cannot bring a charge against us.

In truth we are the righteousness of God in Christ Jesus (2 Cor. 5:21). It is vital that we know that fact, because it is the prayers of a righteous man that will avail much (James 5:16). We have to know that we have been made the righteousness of God. But when we enter into disobedience by refusing to obey the Word, we leave ourselves open for Satan to bring a charge against us. When we follow after the Spirit, and not after the flesh, who can bring a charge against us? It is God who justifies and puts us into right relation to Himself (Rom. 8:33). God does not accuse or impeach those whom He has chosen.

We do not want to leave an opening for Satan's charge, because when we are praying for others, it is with a pure heart that we enforce the laws of the Spirit of life in Christ Jesus, reaffirming the devil's defeat. Known sin in our life strips us of confidence toward God and of the assurance in His divine ability to exercise power and authority over the enemy.

8

Prayer Strategy

Prayer is a spiritual business to be practiced according to God's plan. As we have read in Ephesians 6, there are various types of prayer, or as stated in verse 18, "all manner of prayer and entreaty." The Holy Spirit knows the particular prayer strategy that is needed for any given situation. When we submit to His control, we will pray the appropriate prayer, whether it is an entreaty, supplication, petition, intercession or thanksgiving. If I don't know the prayer strategy needed, I worship and praise my God knowing that praise will stop and still the avenger (Ps. 8 and 9).

The book of Nehemiah reveals the need for the appropriate strategy. After hearing about the needs of his people and the broken walls of Jerusalem, Nehemiah left his prominent position as the royal cup-bearer in the Persian court and went to Jerusalem.

He devised a plan and persuaded the people to rebuild the walls of the Holy City, and while they built the walls, the Lord fought their battles. Every builder had his sword girded by his side while he worked. They were ready to answer the sound of the trumpet. Likewise, we are equipped, ready to answer the call to prayer.

Today, just as in Nehemiah's time, the battle is the Lord's. Since that time Jesus has entered history, establishing the overthrow of Satan. If this is true, why do we have to wage any kind of spiritual warfare, and what is the nature of this warfare?

Sometimes wars were fought to obtain certain rights and establish certain laws. Our victory has already been won. God's laws are already on the books. In a sense you and I are like the governing civil authorities that must now enforce these laws in the land. It is our duty to stand against all enemies who would resist and set themselves up in opposition to God's laws. God has delegated to us the power and authority to enforce His divine will in the earth.

The policeman, for example, has been delegated power and authority. He is not a terror to people of good conduct, but to those who break the law, he is someone to be feared. Satan and his subjects are the lawless spirits who are constantly trying to overthrow the kingdom of God. They are terrified of the children of God who know their delegated power and authority—those who understand the power in the name of Jesus.

Satan's reign as the prince of the power of the air is only for a season; he keeps attempting to overthrow the kingdom of God with guerrilla warfare through deception. Sometimes we have to address these enemy forces just as Jesus did when the devil tempted Him. Jesus is our example. He responded to temptation by declaring the written Word of God. Today, we are the administrators of the victory which was won by our Lord and Savior Jesus Christ when He spoiled principalities and powers, making a show of them openly (Col. 2:15 KJV). As spiritual administrators we must walk in the ways of our Commander.

A Priesthood Which Has Obtained Mercy

As believers you and I are to God a holy and royal priesthood which has obtained mercy. First Peter 2:9-10 KJV tells us:

But ye are a chosen generation, a royal priesthood, an holy nation, a peculiar people; that ye should shew forth the praises of him who hath called you out of darkness into his marvellous light: which in time past were not a people, but are now the people of God: which had not obtained mercy, but now have obtained mercy.

We have obtained God's mercy in the time of our need. I know that you can look back through your life and see how often the mercy of God was extended to you. You weren't even aware that God was looking out for you.

Because of God's mercy and His grace, we are here today seeking to know more about Him and His workings. Through Jesus you and I have obtained mercy and are admonished to be merciful. Jesus rebuked James and John when they wanted to call down fire from heaven upon a village which would not welcome or receive Him (Luke 9:53,54). Isn't this the feeling we have many times when praying for loved ones who do not seem to be responding to the Gospel? God does not want us to call down destruction and calamity on those for whom we pray. Instead, we are to release God's mercy, drawing sinners to Him with bands of love.

Manifesting Mercy and Patience

In Romans 1 and 2, after his characterization of apostates, Paul uttered a profound rebuke, which I believe we should heed. It appears to be a plea for the believer to show mercy rather than disdain and contempt for heretics.

Certainly ungodliness is inexcusable and God's judgment is against sin, but He is not against the sinner. God was merciful and patient toward us while we were yet His enemies (Rom. 5:8). Now He is requesting that we manifest that same mercy and patience to others.

Paul writes on this subject:

"Well," you may be saying, "what terrible people you have been talking about!" But wait a minute! You are just as bad. When you say they are wicked and should be punished, you are talking about yourselves, for you do these very same things. And we know that God, in justice, will punish anyone who does such things as these. Do you think that God will judge and condemn others for doing them and overlook you when you do them, too? Don't you realize how patient he is being with you? Or don't you care? Can't you see that he has been waiting all this time without punishing you, to give you time to turn from your sin? His kindness is meant to lead you to repentance.

Romans 2:1-4 TLB

In Romans 3, Paul continues to build his dissertation with this statement: *For all have sinned, and come short of the glory of God* (Rom. 3:23 KJV). How can we afford to withhold mercy when we were once blind in our sins and in bondage to the god of this world?

Anyone who responds to the goodness of Jesus can be declared "not guilty"; all can be saved by trusting Him to cleanse them from sin. We can all be justified freely by His grace. In Matthew 5:7 KJV, Jesus said, *Blessed are the merciful: for they shall obtain mercy.*

It is impossible to pray effectively for those we are yet holding in contempt. Our cry should be, "Father, forgive them; they know not what they do." Release the mercy of God to those for whom you pray—not judgment and condemnation.

Interceding for a Loved One

When I first began to pray for our son's deliverance from the drug scene, I had little understanding about praying for a third party. I applied the rules governing the prayer of faith to the prayer of intercession.

I had heard that if I prayed more than once for anything, I was praying in doubt and unbelief. However, the Holy Spirit had placed my son David upon my heart, and I found myself praying for him again and again. It is possible for a mother's natural love to turn into unforgiveness, but the love of God will sustain her, enabling her to forgive again and again. A parent's emotions run the gamut from feelings of intense love to feelings of overwhelming acrimony. Sometimes a mother's prayers will be very objective; other times they will be filled with fervent, passionate longing to see that child cleansed by the blood of Jesus.

When praying for a loved one, it is imperative that you admit to yourself and to the Father the emotional hurts, disappointments, fears and anger which so often have been denied. Denial of these emotional feelings hinders answered prayer.

There were times when circumstances looked good and I relaxed my intercession for David, only to have to go back and pray him out of adverse circumstances again. In moments of anger I declared that I would never pray for him again, only to find myself drawn once more by the Holy Spirit to a place of fervent prayer and travail. Such intense intercession is a time for speaking truly and living truly, casting down imaginations and lofty things that seek to exalt themselves above the knowledge of God.

Repeated Intercession

One morning while I was praying, I had a vision of a hedge made up of people and angels with flaming swords surrounding David. Yet I still could not understand why the same prayers had to be repeated. It was in the book of Nehemiah where the Father revealed to me how an addictive person can continually bounce back and forth from compulsive behavior to freedom until he receives emotional wholeness enabling him to overcome toxic addiction.

Let me give you an example of the kind of stability that is required. While Nehemiah was working on the wall, his enemies gathered together, calling him to come down to the plain of Ono and reason with them. But he refused, saying, "I am doing a great work, so I can't come down" (Neh. 6:1-4). Nehemiah made a decision that kept him safe.

However, David's reaction to his tempters was quite different. Our prayers did not override David's free will. But when he would go down to the enemy territory, it was the intercession of the saints that would draw him back within the hedge again.

Often the Holy Spirit alerts me to a need for a particular prayer strategy.

It is true that I am an ordinary, weak human being, but I don't use human plans and methods to win my battles. I use God's mighty weapons, not those made by men, to knock down the devil's strongholds. These weapons can break down every proud argument

against God and every wall that can be built
to keep men from finding him. With these
weapons I can capture rebels and bring them
back to God and change them into men
whose hearts' desire is obedience to Christ.

2 Corinthians 10:3-5 TLB

We don't give up; God is able and willing to give us another start.

Strongholds must be pulled down. When I set myself to persevere in prayer for our son, I found myself in a spiritual battle, a tug of war. Satan does not want to relinquish even one individual he is holding in bondage.

Reasoning with David only made him more stubborn. He resolved that his parents would not tell him how to live his life. He was a rock and nothing could move him. It was as though his intellect had disappeared, and we heard statements that defied all logic.

Obviously, David had taken leave of his senses—he was no longer in his right mind. Was this the son we had loved and raised? Many times it appeared that the enemy had won. But I knew in whom I believed, and I was persuaded that my household would be saved.

In Matthew 18 Jesus gave the keys of binding and loosing to the church, but for a long time I didn't understand how to use these keys effectively. If binding the devil works, or if loosing the devil works, he should have been bound and loosed most definitely because I did both. God will move heaven and earth to give you the understanding concerning the necessary spiritual weapons for the needed prayer strategy.

In *Shattering Your Strongholds,* Liberty Savard gives a basic outline for binding and loosing prayers for your unsaved loved ones. She writes:

> "To hold them steady, I bind (the positive, helpful side of binding) the individual to the will of God, the truth, the blood of Jesus, the mind of Christ and the work of the cross. I bind the strong man, Satan, (the negative, restraining side of binding) and then loose, crush, destroy, shatter, melt and tear apart all hindrances, devices and influences he is trying to bring against the individual.

> The next step is to tear down the strongholds in the lives of the captives. This is vital to keep them from cooperating with the enemy's attempts to recapture them. You can pull them out of the fire, but you have to continue loosing their strongholds to keep them from voluntarily returning there. Continue loosing until the Holy Spirit reveals they have begun to take over the reins of their own deliverance."[1]

Continue to build up the wall and stand in the gap before God. Don't turn coward, lose heart and give up! All things are possible to him who believes. If your faith seems weak, cry out, "Lord, help my unbelief." He will help you. He sent the Holy Spirit to be your Strengthener and Standby. He is interceding.

The words that you speak are creative and will not return to God void. Never be moved by good or bad circumstances, but keep your anchor firmly grounded in the Word of God. Remain steady regardless of the situation. Don't give up your position of priesthood or abort the mission which God has placed on your heart. You will know through the witness of the Holy Spirit when you have fulfilled your assignment. There will be a definite release within you—a knowing that you must experience personally in order to completely understand. Pray, extending forgiveness, obtaining mercy and grace, until the work is accomplished.

A Burden for Prayer

I well remember an incident from my teenage years which demonstrates a temporary "burden" for prayer.

Our family had gone to visit my grandparents and we were returning home when we had a brush with death. The next day one of the church members called my dad to inquire if our lives had been in danger at a certain moment. He said that about that time God had awakened him, and our faces had flashed before him as he prayed with groanings in the Spirit.

In this case, the Father found someone who responded to His call, someone who was faithful to pray, protecting us from an accident which could have snuffed out our lives. This man fulfilled his role as a priest unto God on behalf of his pastor and his family in time of crisis.

God wants your prayer time devoted to situations outside of your own personal problems. Develop the mind of Christ within you, holding the thoughts, feelings and purposes of His heart.

A Sweet-Smelling Fragrance

In the tabernacle of the Old Testament, which was a place of worship, an altar of incense stood in the inner court. Incense was burned upon the altar morning and evening. It was symbolic of acceptable prayers.

In the New Testament this altar is now placed just before the throne of God. When you come before God, you come into His throne room, presenting yourself before His throne. Your prayers are a sweet-smelling fragrance before God. They are a perpetual and continual flow before the Lord, because prayer is persevering. Jesus said to pray without ceasing. I would venture to say that most every prayer you have ever prayed is in the throne room as incense before the Lord.

Broaden Your Vision

The Holy Spirit desires to broaden the scope of your prayer life. The Father has a plan for humankind and He desires that you become involved in this plan. He wants you to expand your prayer borders beyond the confines of your home and your local church. (However, do not neglect these vital areas of prayer.)

In Psalm 2:8 KJV the Father said, *Ask of me, and I shall give thee the heathen for thine inheritance, and the uttermost parts of the earth for thy possession.* Expand your vision. Allow the Lord to imprint His intercession on the tablets of your heart, delegating prayer assignments to you as He wills. He wants you to become kingdom-minded in preparation for the return of Jesus. Expand your prayer vision to include nations. Get beyond the needs of your family as well as those prayer situations in the local church.

Pray for the will of God to be done on earth as it is in heaven. Problems should not dictate your prayer life. As you carry out your prayer assignments, submit to the leadership of the Spirit of God. Whether it is for the family, the church, the community or the nation, remain faithful to your assigned prayer burden until it is fulfilled.

Agree With the Plans and Purposes of God

Involve yourself in the things that Jesus is doing. You were destined from the beginning to be molded into the image of God's Son (Rom. 8:29). Act like Jesus. Walk like Jesus. Talk like Jesus. Adopt the same attitude and purpose which was in Christ Jesus (Phil. 2:5). In His present-day ministry, Jesus is the High Priest who intercedes before God the Father.

Seeing then that we have a great high priest, that is passed into the heavens, Jesus the Son of God, let us hold fast our profession.

Hebrews 4:14 KJV

In Greek the word translated "profession" is *homologia,* which means, "agreement; terms of surrender,"[2] or "confession."[3] Let us meet the terms of surrender to God by affirming our faith in Him and His Word. This requires agreement with the plans and purposes of God.

For we have not an high priest which cannot
be touched with the feeling of our infirmities;
but was in all points tempted like as we are,
yet without sin.

Hebrews 4:15 KJV

According to W.E. Vine, "infirmities" means "want of strength,...weakness,...inability to produce results."[4]

Many times in prayer we experience an inability to produce results, but Jesus is touched with these infirmities. According to Matthew 8:17, He bore these weaknesses, and in Romans 8:26 we find that we have a Helper Who takes hold together with us against these inabilities in order to produce results. Jesus has made us "kings and priests" unto God the Father (Rev. 1:6 KJV).

As new covenant believers you and I are part of "an holy priesthood" (offering up spiritual sacrifices, acceptable to God by Jesus Christ) and a "royal priesthood" that we should show forth the praises of Him who has called us out of darkness into His marvelous light (1 Peter 2:5,9 KJV). The first ministry of a New Testament priest is to offer up praises to God; the second is to declare His wonderful salvation through a life which emulates Jesus.

When we who are priests under the new covenant pray here on earth, our High Priest presents our petitions before the Father.

A Successful Prayer Life

Examination of the lives of prominent Christian men and women reveals that they were, and are, men and women of prayer. Jesus has given us believers a pattern for successful living, which includes a successful prayer life.

In the Song of Solomon 2:13,14 a superb passage of Scripture calls us into a wonderful relationship with our Lord. The bridegroom (representing Christ) says to his beloved bride:

Arise, my love, my fair one, and come away.
Let me see your face, let me hear your voice;
for your voice is sweet, and your face is
lovely.

This is the call of Jesus to the church today: "Arise, come apart, come away with Me." Everyone who spends time with Jesus discovers divine plans and purposes for his life. *The Lord confides in those who fear him; he makes his covenant known to them* (Ps. 25:14 NIV). What has God placed on your heart? The

Christian's prayer armor is of the Spirit, and God has written certain prayer ventures on your breastplate.

A sincere desire to have a successful prayer life necessitates looking beyond situations, problems and circumstances. Don't be afraid of prayer burdens. Jesus said, *My yoke is easy, and my burden is light* (Matt. 11:30 KJV). Paul wrote:

> *For our light affliction, which is but for a moment, worketh for us a far more exceeding and eternal weight of glory; while we look not at the things which are seen, but at the things which are not seen: for the things which are seen are temporal; but the things which are not seen are eternal.*
>
> 2 Corinthians 4:17,18 KJV

Situations in this world are constantly changing, but the things of the Spirit are unchanging. Involve yourself with the intercession of Jesus. Become utterly one with Him.

Jesus, Our Foundation

God has said that His house would be called a house of prayer (Isa. 56:7; Matt. 21:13). You and I are that habitation with a firm and sure foundation. In 1 Corinthians 3:11 we find that no man can lay a foundation other than the one which is laid, Jesus Christ. So, as our Foundation and High Priest, Jesus is our backing for all prayer, including spiritual warfare.

The church was a mystery in the Old Testament, but today we are the church. Isaiah prophesied about the church when he said:

> *Therefore thus says the Lord God, "Behold, I am laying in Zion a stone, a tested stone, a costly cornerstone for the foundation, firmly placed."*

Isaiah 28:16 NAS

Jesus, our Foundation and Builder, says, "The gates of hell shall not prevail against you" (Matt. 16:18 KJV). Hallelujah! When we enter a spiritual battle we are not trying to obtain the victory. God has given us the victory, and *this is the victory that overcometh the world, even our faith* (1 John 5:4).

You are ready to assume your responsibility in the household of faith, knowing that you are a winner, more than a conqueror and called to a lifestyle of prayer. You belong to a holy and royal priesthood.

9

The Good Fight of Faith

Timothy, my son, I give you this instruction in keeping with the prophecies once made about you, so that by following them you may fight the good fight, holding on to faith and a good conscience. Some have rejected these and so have shipwrecked their faith.

1 Timothy 1:18,19 NIV

Prayer is not mystical or ethereal. God Himself is practical in His instructions for living the more abundant life, which includes communication with God through prayer.

He has not left us to wander aimlessly around, hoping to stumble onto proper prayer techniques. He is a loving Father who knows how to reveal His ways to those who will abide in His presence.

Assuredly, the Bible speaks of "warfare." To wage this fight, which Paul calls a "good warfare," each one must cling tightly to his faith in God's Word and maintain a clear conscience.

Spiritual Weapons

Paul again speaks of this warfare in 2 Corinthians 10:3-4 NIV:

> *For though we live in the world, we do not wage war as the world does. The weapons we fight with are not the weapons of the world. On the contrary, they have divine power to demolish strongholds.*

These spiritual weapons are for the demolition of enemy strongholds—mental barriers and imaginations or human reasoning programmed by philosophy, religious dogmas, childish suppositions and ideas fashioned after and adapted to this world's external, superficial customs. These proud arguments and obstacles are fortifications that have set themselves up against the knowledge of God.

The true intercessor refuses to be conformed to this world, but is transformed by the renewing of his mind, that he *may prove what is that good, and acceptable, and perfect, will of God* (Rom. 12:2 KJV).

This is required if we truly present our bodies as living sacrifices unto God, which is our reasonable service and worship (Rom. 12:1). We must bring our thoughts into obedience to the Captain of our salvation.

I will use these weapons against every rebel who remains after I have first used them on myself and have surrendered to Christ.

Building Up Through Worship

It is imperative that we keep ourselves built up through worship. God is looking for true worshipers—those who will worship Him in spirit and in truth (John 4:24). Worship keeps us secure in the secret place of the Most High.

A thousand may fall at your side, and ten thousand at your right hand, but it shall not come near you.

Only a spectator shall you be [yourself inaccessible in the secret place of the Most High] as you witness the reward of the wicked.

Because you have made the Lord your refuge, and the Most High your dwelling place, there shall no evil befall you, nor any plague or calamity come near your tent.

Psalm 91:7-10

You do not have to be afraid of the enemy's tactics. Continually throughout the Word of God we read, "Do not fear," "Be not afraid," "Be of good courage." You do not have to fear that demons will jump on you or attach themselves to you. Fear opens the door for demonic activity; faith is your shield that will *quench all the flaming missiles of the wicked [one]* (Eph. 6:16). You are inaccessible in the secret place of the Most High.

Maintain an attitude of worship by acknowledging the presence of God at all times. His praise is to be continually in your mouth.

Recognize the Enemy

There was a time when I treated my husband as though he were my enemy. Before I learned to pray prayers that avail much, as I mentioned before, I tried every tactic that I knew to force him to go to church. After all, this was certainly the will of God. He needed to be a good example to our children and, besides that, I was tired of always feeling so alone.

Every Sunday morning the battleground was set. I woke up the children, fed them breakfast and saw that they got dressed properly while my husband remained in bed. At every opportunity I ran to the bedroom nagging, coercing, speaking gently and screaming, among other things. Sometimes I would wake the children early and send them into the bedroom to wake Daddy.

One day the Holy Spirit said to me, "Since you have prayed, believe." The gentle voice of the Spirit instructed me to treat my husband just as I would if he were attending church. I realized that believing is acting as though God has heard and answered prayer. This is action added to faith.

Sunday mornings were certainly easier for the children and me once I changed my behavior through the grace given me by the Lord Jesus. My prayers prevailed when I submitted to God, allowing Him to work His will in me. I yelled a big loud no at the devil and watched him scamper (James 4:7). It was only a few weeks later that I walked into the living room and saw my husband dressed, announcing that he was going to church with us.

The Devices of Satan

Ephesians 6:10-18, which describes our prayer armor and lists our weapons of prayer, exposes the enemy and his ranks. Paul begins in verse 10 by giving believers an exhortation to develop and exercise the courage necessary to resist and stand against the enemies of God.

These unseen enemies are trying to turn us from the Lord; to create fear, doubt and unbelief; to coerce us into being unfaithful to God's Word. Satan uses deceit, pressure and cunning craftiness as snares set to keep our attention on problems, provoking us to believe that other people are to blame for our circumstances.

Our insecurities allow Satan to send us thoughts of accusation against people. Much too often we cling to our unhealed hurts and unresolved personal issues. In an effort to protect ourselves, we camouflage the deep, crippled emotions with a proud look, a lying tongue, hands that shed innocent blood, a heart that devises wicked imaginations, feet that are quick to rush into evil and a false witness that speaks lies (Prov. 6:17). We have the necessary weapons to pull down strongholds of suspicion, unforgiveness and distrust that incite us to hurl accusations at one another, sowing discord among the brethren. We have been called to freedom, but we must not allow freedom to become an incentive to our flesh or an excuse for selfishness; rather, it gives us the opportunity to serve one another in love (Gal. 5:13).

Satan's greatest delight is to disturb harmony. One of his favorite ploys is heaping condemnation on the believer, turning him against himself. Paul makes it clear that we are not to be against one another or ourselves, but against spiritual rebels in heavenly places.

Wrestling Against Spiritual Enemies

Finally, my brethren, be strong in the Lord, and in the power of his might. Put on the whole armour of God, that ye may be able to stand against the wiles of the devil. For we wrestle not against flesh and blood, but against principalities, against powers, against the rulers of the darkness of this world, against spiritual wickedness in high places.

Ephesians 6:10-12 KJV

Jesus knew that there would be people who would not accept us, but who would set themselves against the Word of God, which we preach. Yet He said to us, *Love your enemies, bless them that curse you, do good to them that hate you, and pray for them which despitefully use you, and persecute you* (Matt. 5:44 KJV). Our Lord was never against a person, only against the evil one who holds people in bondage.

Paul's writings are in harmony with the teachings of Jesus. Here in Ephesians he says that we are not to wrestle against people, or to set ourselves against them, but that our battle is against Satan. So, what is the practical application of this Scripture? How does one wrestle with the devil?

One day while searching for the true meaning of this word *wrestle* in *Vine's Expository Dictionary*, I came across two seemingly insignificant shades of meaning: "sway" and "vibrate." Mr. Vine wrote that "wrestling...is used figuratively, in Ephesians 6:12, of the spiritual conflict engaged in by believers."[1]

The two synonyms given made no sense to me. I tried out, "We *sway* not against flesh and blood," and then, "We *vibrate* not against flesh and blood." It appeared that these two words simply did not work in that context.

When I would call up a mental image of the word *wrestle,* my mind would immediately present a picture of two massive men in various holds, each trying to pin the other down for the count of three. I realized that if Jesus had not defeated Satan, I would have been in big trouble. Somehow I could not see myself in this kind of struggle with the devil.

However, mental images of the words *sway* and *vibrate* didn't bring any acceptable revelation. I knew that Scripture must interpret Scripture. The only swaying I could think of that would appear scriptural was that of the trees planted by the rivers of living waters in Psalm 1 (which, the text tells us, are firmly planted), which could be a representation of believers as they are buffeted by the storms and winds. That seemed pretty good. It illustrated the fact that we cannot be uprooted. But somehow I knew that there was more to be understood.

According to Webster's dictionary, to *sway* means "to swing or move from side to side, or to and fro—to vacillate or alternate between one position or opinion and another."[2] Some believers try to function in this mind-set, swaying back and forth between different kinds of teaching, or being "double minded" as James calls it (James 1:8 KJV), and thus receiving nothing from God. They grow weary in their prayer life and many of them faint in their minds.

However, there is another meaning of this word *sway*. It also means "to rule, to reign, to hold sway; to cause a person, an opinion or actions to be inclined a certain way or be turned from a given course or diverted."[3] Therefore, to *sway* means "to rule over, control, dominate or prevail."

According to Ephesians 1:20-22, we believers are seated in heavenly places in Christ *far above* the earthly realm. Yes, there is spiritual warfare going on all around us, but we hold sway over Satan and his forces. In the name of Jesus, we have the authority, power, might and strength to cause Satan to turn from a given course.

Isn't that what we are trying to do in spiritual warfare—to turn the course of Satan, to divert him from that which he has plotted and planned against the body of Christ? In spiritual warfare we hold sway over him, not over human beings; we have authority and control over principalities, powers, the rulers of the darkness of this world and spiritual wickedness in heavenly places.

In one place the psalmist said, "It's as though we were dreaming" (Ps. 126:1). Of course, he was speaking of the captives' release from slavery, but it is almost too good to be true—you and I have power and authority over the evil one.

Church, let's awaken, stop our moaning and groaning about the wiles of the devil and assume our place of spiritual authority, behaving like sons and daughters of the Most High God.

Vibrating Light or Wavering Opinion?

What about the word *vibrate?* According to Webster it means "to give off light or sound by vibration."[4] A vibration is an emotional quality or supernatural emanation that is sensed by another person or thing.

The world talks about walking into a room and sensing "vibes." I know that havoc must take place in the seat of Satan's empire as we believers stand clothed in the armor of light, praying all manner of prayer. Light dispels darkness. John wrote, *And the Light shines on in the darkness, for the darkness has never overpowered it [put it out or absorbed it or appropriated it, and is unreceptive to it]* (John 1:5). Jesus said to His disciples, *Ye are the light of the world* (Matt. 5:14 KJV). Paul wrote, *For once you were darkness, but now you are light in the Lord; walk as children of Light* (Eph. 5:8).

Another meaning of *vibrate* is "to vacillate or waver as between two opinions"[5] (that is, between belief and doubt, faith and fear). This frustrates the purposes and plans of God's prayer agenda. Swaying or vacillating between two opinions is the result of the presence of strongholds which have not yet been pulled down. *The weapons of our warfare are not carnal, but mighty through God to the pulling down of strong holds* (2 Cor. 10:4 KJV).

How do we "sway" and "vibrate" against spiritual rebels? By putting on the whole armor of God and praying at all times—on every occasion, in every season—in the Spirit, with all manner of prayer and entreaty (Eph. 6:18). We can also "sway" the enemy by speaking God's Word and praying with the understanding. God's Word is our sword, and when the enemy comes to destroy our homes, churches and communities, we remind him of his defeat at Calvary by affirming God's Word over everything that concerns us.

The entrance of God's Word brings light and dispells darkness (Ps. 119:130). When Jesus was confronted by Satan, He declared, "It is written," quoting from the Old Testament Scriptures (Luke 4). Turn to the Word of God for answers. Affirm the Word in your meditation and through prayer. There is no better prayer book. God is watching over His Word to perform it (Jer. 1:12).

10

The Overthrow of Satan

It is evident that Satan is still at work to deceive, accuse, divide and overthrow the church of the Lord Jesus Christ. The church is a sleeping giant, awakening to the truth of the utter defeat of Satan.

Jesus spoiled principalities and powers, making a show of them openly, exposing Satan to public shame (Col. 2:15). In Genesis 3:15 KJV the Lord revealed that the enemy would "bruise the heel" (a metaphor for temporary suffering) of the Seed of the woman, while promising that the Seed was to utterly crush and eternally defeat Satan. Little did Satan know that the death of Jesus would be his absolute defeat.

It is imperative to successfully stand against rebel forces, that we understand the victory that was fought and won by our Redeemer who conquered Satan by dying for us. In Colossians 2:15 NIV, Paul reveals the absolute defeat of the devil by Jesus Christ: *And having disarmed the powers and authorities, he made a public spectacle of them, triumphing over them by the cross.*

Now, God, through Christ Jesus, through the Cross, has already disarmed principalities and powers. In 1 Corinthians 2:8 we find that if the prince of this world had known what was going to happen, he would never have crucified the Son of God. In that Crucifixion came his defeat.

The Location of Jesus

Paul then receives the divine revelation of how Jesus utterly defeated Satan, his principalities and powers. We have shared in an earlier chapter our relationship to our Commander in Chief and to our enemy. Again we will locate Jesus, Satan and the church. We need to have an understanding of where we are all located in the spirit realm in order to carry on strategic prayer assignments. We will locate Jesus first.

In Ephesians 1:20-23 NIV we find Paul referring to the power of God:

[It was this power] *which he exerted in Christ when he raised him from the dead and seated him at his right hand in the heavenly realms* [where?], *far above all rule and authority, power and dominion, and every title that can be given, not only in the present age but also in the one to come. And God placed all things under his feet and appointed him to be head over everything for the church, which is his body, the fullness of him who fills everything in every way.*

The physical location of the Lord Jesus today is at the right hand of the Father, where He sits in glory as the spiritual Head of the church.

Location of the Church

It is also vital that we understand our spiritual location. In Ephesians 2 we find that we were once children of disobedience, objects of wrath and under the control of the prince of the power of the air (Satan). We were powerless to deliver ourselves from this bondage. But God, who is rich in mercy, made us alive with Christ, raised us up with Him and seated us with Him in the heavenly realms (Eph. 2:4-6). So, where are we located? In Christ! Where is that? If we are truly in Him, then we are seated *far above* all principality, and power, and might, and dominion and every name that is named not only in this world, but also in that which is to come.

This elevated status does not put us in a position to lord it over people but in a position to be the delegated authority in the world of the spirit. It appears to me that we already hold the keys to victory; we already have the victory since we are already seated with Christ in heavenly places. That means that Satan is somewhere out there, and when we locate him, we find that he is a defeated foe—underneath the feet of Jesus.

It seems almost too good to be true when we begin to comprehend the position of the body of Christ. Often our mental image has been one that suggests that Satan is just barely under our feet and we are actually treading on him. This is not the picture we get from Ephesians where we find that we are seated far *above* the satanic regime.

Our Lord won a decisive battle—not just a skirmish that gives us limited authority over the enemy, but a *total victory* that renders the devil paralyzed (Heb. 2:14,15).

Even before the death and resurrection of Jesus, He sent His disciples out, saying, *Behold! I have given you authority and power to trample upon serpents and scorpions, and [physical and mental strength and ability] over all the power that the enemy [possesses]; and nothing shall in any way harm you* (Luke 10:19).

Jesus gave them physical and mental strength and ability to carry out the work that He had begun while here on earth. Jesus went about in the towns and villages teaching in synagogues and preaching the Good News of the kingdom and healing every disease and every weakness and infirmity among the people (Matt. 4:24). Then in John 14:12 NIV He said to His disciples: *"I tell you the truth, anyone who has faith in me will do what I have been doing. He will do even greater things than these, because I am going to the Father."*

You and I are to do the works of Jesus, knowing that the prayers of a righteous man avail much. Jesus knew that there would be opposition to the Gospel and that His people would suffer persecution, but He wants you *and* me to know that the defeat of Satan was effective and we are to keep it in effect.

The Location of Satan

Even before His death, burial and Resurrection, Jesus gave His disciples power over the enemy in His name. Are we to suppose that now, after the Resurrection, the church has less power that these men had before the Cross? Never! How dare we continue to glorify the works of the devil with our proclamations and testimonies and, in some cases, our fears.

Satan is a defeated foe. The prophet Isaiah says that we will look at Satan and say, "You mean this is the man who shook the earth and made kingdoms tremble?" (Isa. 14:16). When we realize that Satan's power and authority over the church of the Lord Jesus have really been broken and put to naught, we will begin to be even more effective in our prayers.

We can see from the passage in Luke that Satan does not have authority over the children of God. His only weapon is deception through fear. Let's change our focus from the works of Satan to the wondrous works of God, for He has done great things.

It was Nehemiah who said to the people of his day, "Don't be afraid; the Lord will fight your battles" (Neh. 4:14). If the Lord would do that for those under the old covenant, how much more would He desire to do that for us who are under the new covenant? This is not because He cares for us more than He cared for ancient Israel, whom He called the apple of His eye, but because of what was accomplished through the Cross.

Hebrews 2:14-15 NIV is an exciting, bold statement about Jesus Christ.

Since the children have flesh and blood, he too shared in their humanity so that by his death he might destroy him who holds the power of death—that is, the devil—and free those who all their lives were held in slavery by their fear of death.

Jesus has made Satan of no effect and has brought him to naught. Jesus paid a debt He did not owe. We could not get out of our bondage on our own, but Jesus came on our behalf. He dealt a fatal blow to Satan that made him of no effect and delivered us out of bondage. That which was impossible for humans was possible with God.

Satan works through deceit, through confusion of the minds of people. In order to pursue his destruction on the earth, he has to have human cooperation. To accomplish his earthly deeds, he needs physical bodies.

Sin begins with a thought (James 1:14). Where does discord begin in our homes and churches? It begins with a thought. When that thought is considered valid, we begin a progressive search to prove its validity. Thoughts against others; feelings of rejection, intimidation, insecurity; the belief that others are against us; high-minded attitudes which convince us that we are better than others, causing us to overestimate ourselves and underestimate others—all such mental activity is contrary to truth. The next thing we know, we are speaking out what we are thinking, and those words begin to build fires among our co-workers, friends and companions. Then everything gets out of hand and we can't imagine how it all began. The result of wrong thinking is strife and every evil work.

Responsibility in the Church

Division is in the church, the home, the community and the office. It pits brother against brother, pastor against his congregation, congregation against pastor. Spouse against spouse, children against parent and vice versa. Mother-in-law against daughter-in-law, boss against employee and employee against boss. Strife and discord affect everyone.

What is our responsibility as the body of Christ, those "lively stones" about whom Peter wrote? As living stones we have a part to play in the church of Jesus Christ. God did not create passive stones; He created lively stones. We are to exercise all the power that He has given us in the spirit realm. Our heavenly Father has given us power to be creative in this world, to exert a positive influence, to make a difference in the cities and towns in which we are planted.

All of us are to make a difference in our churches, in our neighborhoods, and in our businesses and homes. I want to remind you once again that Jesus said that the gates of hell shall not prevail against us. Sometimes it looks as if God has got a lot to do to make that statement come true. Sometimes it looks as if the gates of hell are prevailing. That is when our faith comes into the picture. By faith we reach out and take hold of what Jesus said: "The gates of hell shall not prevail against *you!*" (Matt. 16:18).

11

Life in the Prayer Closet and Beyond

Now that your prayer foundation and responsibility as a priest have been established, let's look at prayer as a lifestyle both in the prayer closet and beyond.

In Matthew 6, Jesus spoke to His disciples about prayer, saying:

> *And when you pray, do not be like the hypocrites, for they love to pray standing in the synagogues and on the street corners to be seen by men. I tell you the truth, they have received their reward in full. But when you pray, go into your room, close the door and pray to your Father, who is unseen. Then your Father, who sees what is done in secret, will reward you. And when you pray, do not keep on babbling like pagans, for they think they will be heard because of their many*

words. Do not be like them, for your Father knows what you need before you ask him.

Matthew 6:5-8 NIV

Then in verses 9 through 13 Jesus gives us a prayer outline, commonly known as the Lord's Prayer. He continues His teaching on prayer with these words:

For if you forgive men when they sin against you, your heavenly Father will also forgive you. But if you do not forgive men their sins, your Father will not forgive your sins.

Matthew 6:14,15 NIV

In this passage Jesus connects prayer and forgiveness, an essential ingredient in the development of healthy relationships. Prayer enables us to pull down strongholds which prohibit unity in private households as well as in the household of God.

Major Strongholds

Paul tells us that *the weapons of our warfare are not carnal, but mighty through God to the pulling down of strong holds* (2 Cor. 10:4 KJV). Strongholds, places of security or survival, are established in the mind. Many of these were developed during childhood as defenses against imaginary or actual dangerous emotional or physical situations. Even though our perceptions of events which took place may have been perverted and distorted, the strongholds are real. If carried over into adulthood, they sabotage what otherwise could be good, healthy relationships.

The tragedy is that past hurts and disappointments often lead to unforgiveness, which is the greatest hindrance to answered prayer. Jesus spent most of His ministry preaching about the logistics of human relationships. He told His followers, *And whenever you stand praying, if you have anything against any one, forgive him and let it drop (leave it, let it go), in order that your Father Who is in heaven may also forgive you your [own] failings and shortcomings and let them drop* (Mark 11:25).

I know that you have experienced those times when you have talked with someone who could neither hear nor understand what you were saying. Later you discovered that you had not heard the other person accurately either. You have come up against a stronghold or mind-set. These strongholds interfere with the voice of the Holy Spirit and divert us from the purpose and will of God in our prayer life, causing us to pray according to our own wishes. We do not hear what the Spirit is saying; we do not understand His direction.

If your heart is truly after the things of God, then the Holy Spirit does not give up on you. He sends you the truth that enables you to pull down every stronghold and cast *down imaginations, and every high thing that exalteth itself against the knowledge of God* (2 Cor. 10:5 KJV).

The enemy uses our strongholds of ignorance, prejudices, lusts, imaginations, carnal reasoning and pride (1 John 2:16). Our prayers must be according to the will of God, not according to imaginations and unhealthy mind-sets based on "doing our own thing," or instant gratification of our material desires.

Life Beyond the Prayer Closet

Life in the prayer closet can ensure a successful life beyond the prayer closet. God is interested in His children developing character and healthy relationships, for then we can *give attentive, continuous care to watching over one another, studying how we may stir up (stimulate and incite) to love and helpful deeds and noble activities* (Heb. 10:24). These relationships are born out of a productive prayer life.

Our prayers must not be based on misconceptions and false perceptions. We should never try to manipulate the lives of others or insist on changing them according to our own desires.

Our strongholds of rigidity, denial, emotional isolation and silence must be recognized, broken down and confessed in repentance to God the Father. *Rigidity* renders a person inflexible, suppressing the ministry of our constant transformation. *Denial* opens the door for self-deception, repudiating the truth which sets us free. *Emotional isolation* causes us to be subject to hardness of heart, overruling our compassion for others. *Silence* stops the communication of our faith, hindering our true fellowship with God and man.

The Holy Spirit brings revelation, Jesus breaks down every wall, and our heavenly Father restores and brings salvation to our every destruction. He always wants you and me to be aware that we represent Him right where we live and wherever He sends us. These strongholds inhibit good communication skills and hinder our testimony of a life of peace and victory.

There is a life in the prayer closet and beyond. In Matthew 6 Jesus teaches on the subject of prayer. He warns us about behaving as hypocrites who love to make a show of their religiosity. Jesus teaches us to go into the prayer closet and promises that our Father, Who sees in secret, will reward us openly. "Going into the prayer closet" is easily understood. Most conscientious believers are willing to follow these instructions about praying privately. How does God reward us openly? I believe that most of us who have prayed diligently for our families would say that our reward is noticeable behavioral changes in our loved ones.

God desires to bring about changes in our homes as well as to develop within us the desire to live as mature followers of our Lord Jesus Christ. That which is openly manifested in us should be the fruit of the Spirit, those godly characteristics which influence others and draw them to Jesus Christ.

What does my behavior reflect to those with whom I come in contact? Do I wear my prayer life as a badge of self-righteousness as if I were the only one who had knowledge of what godly behavior is?

God has said that the spouse may be saved by the godly behavior of the believing spouse. What does our behavior say about us? Do we wear our prayer life as a badge, proclaiming either overtly or subconsciously to all about our sacrificial life in the prayer closet; or do we demonstrate righteousness, peace and joy in the Holy Ghost to our loved ones? These are questions that each of us must look at honestly.

It is our responsibility to be sensitive to the voice of God and responsive to His call to intercession both in the prayer closet and beyond. God wants to use us as channels of answered prayer. In our daily lives we exemplify the changes which took place through our diligent prayer time with the Father.

Remember, the seeds of prayer that you have sown on behalf of others will profit you, change your false beliefs, destroy your past defenses and enable you to complete your ministry of reconciliation.

12

Prayer Time: Joy or Bondage?

Today we are hearing testimonies from many who are rising early in the morning to pray. The testimonies are very inspiring as we are told of the benefits of rising early to seek the Lord. Manifold Scriptures are given to support this practice and it seems that everyone who hears gets excited and makes the decision to adapt his or her lifestyle to include early morning prayer time.

How early one gets up to pray has become a topic of conversation in some Christian circles. The emphasis has changed from *praying* to how *early* that praying should be done. Many people are quietly going about obeying God, praying early each day as the Spirit has directed. Some are rising early, even going to their churches, and have experienced great changes in their lives. Among these, however, there are those who have unconsciously become prideful, boasting about their achievement, while others are suffering from self-condemnation, wondering why they have not been able to conquer their sleeping habits.

As many as are led by the Spirit of God, they are the sons of God (Rom. 8:14 KJV). If you believe that God desires you to rise early to keep your appointment with Him, you must obey. However, if you are struggling to meet someone else's expectations, be set free today to follow the Spirit of the Lord.

I believe that you must be led by the Spirit of God concerning both the time and the duration of your prayer sessions.

How long should we pray? Jesus said to His disciples in the Garden of Gethsemane, *Are you so utterly unable to stay awake and keep watch with Me for one hour?* (Matt. 26:40). This statement has become the *rhema* of God to many people and they are praying at least one hour each day. If this verse has not become revelation knowledge to you personally, or if you are just trying to imitate what others are doing, then your prayer time can easily become a drudgery and just another work of the flesh. Prayer is habit-forming. Those who make the decision to pray one hour soon find that time increased. The more you pray, the more you desire to pray.

Christians must submit to the leadership of the Spirit of God in the matter of prayer. I urge you to depend on the Holy Spirit who knows you and your individual personality, lifestyle and schedule. It is He who will instruct you and show you the pathway of prayer that is right for you.

What time should I pray? Is early morning the only time to pray? If I don't get up early to pray, is it a sign that I don't love God as much as I should? Is Satan interfering with my prayer life, stealing my time by making it difficult for me to get out of bed? Will God hear me at 10 A.M., at 1 P.M. or at 9 P.M. as quickly and clearly as He will at 5 A.M.?

Praying out of a sense of guilt or according to another's standards can make prayer a bondage rather than a privilege. For instance, if a person sleeps past his self-appointed hour of prayer, he can easily become consumed with his failure to get out of bed when he was supposed to. A pattern of negative thinking can be immediately set in motion to wreak havoc with his prayer time. Also, if for some reason his allotted prayer time is cut short, he feels guilty and his confidence in God can be shaken for that day.

Does God command everyone to rise before daybreak to pray, regardless of individual and family lifestyles or job situations? I don't think so.

We do need to find time alone with the Father daily, whether it is early in the morning, in the middle of the afternoon or late in the evening. It is easier for me if I begin my day with prayer. The first thing I do upon waking is greet the Father, Jesus and the Holy Spirit. The time is not as important as the circumstances and the state of our own heart and mind.

Several years ago my mom, Donnis Griffin, asked the Holy Spirit to reveal to her a time she could be alone with God. That was not as simple as it may sound because my dad had retired from pastoral work and was always home. But since Mom always says, "Don't ask God a question unless you want to know the answer," she was open to whatever the Lord might present. The Holy Spirit responded by telling her to get up and pray each morning while Dad was out jogging. That was fine, except that he was an early riser, one of those types who believes that when you get up you should be instantly awake all over—spirit, soul and body.

Mom was a late sleeper. However, she had asked the Lord for an answer and got it, so she was determined that she would obey God. Soon she found herself waking up even before Dad because the Lord had created a desire in her to get up and spend time in His presence. Her time alone with God was the most important time of her day. Early morning prayer became a way of life for her. The answers to her prayers were remarkable and caused much thanksgiving to God the Father.

As a result, her fellowship with God grew more and more intimate.

Several years before her death my mother shared this experience with me. I became very excited about it and decided that if she could do that, then so could I. My self-appointed time with God early every morning did not last too long. When I compared lifestyles, I found that Mom was going to bed very early in the evening in order to get up before daylight. However, this early rising had become such a part of her daily routine that even when she was up late at night for some reason, it didn't stop her from rising early the next morning to spend time with God.

As I looked at my schedule, I discovered that my routine was quite different from my mother's. My family and church situations required that I be up late at night more often than not.

Condemnation flooded me again and again as I tried to make myself get up to conform to my mother's routine. "Others get up early for their prayer time, so why can't I?" I asked myself. "What's wrong with me? Why can't I conquer this thing which causes me to sleep past the time everyone else is already praying?"

I felt as though I had failed God when I had not risen early (at 4:30 or 5 A.M.) to pray. If I didn't get up at that time, then I could not get in the number of hours that the others were spending in prayer. For example, my mother prayed until she was through—however long that took. Others were letting me know that they were praying for four to six hours each day and that I was not being obedient to God if I didn't do the same. I felt a burden of guilt and self-condemnation. My mom said that the Holy Spirit gave the schedule to her, and she did not place this burden of guilt on me. She reminded me that I must ask Him to give me my personal schedule for prayer.

In the end, the Father and I worked it out. I now set my clock for a certain hour that is compatible with my lifestyle. However, many mornings the Holy Spirit calls my name before the clock-radio sounds off. Remember that God is effectually at work in you, energizing and creating in you the power and desire both to will and to work for His good pleasure and satisfaction and delight (Phil. 2:13). He will do His part; it is your responsibility to cooperate. *If you are willing and obedient, you shall eat the good of the land* (Isa. 1:19).

The second example is a gentleman here in Atlanta who has been used mightily by God to influence the lives of many people who have frequented his place of business. He has many testimonies to share as a result of prayer and being obedient to the Spirit. He has seen many lives changed, including people who have received salvation and healing. His time to pray is 9 P.M.

If you ask this man to pray for you, you can know that at some point between nine and ten o'clock in the evening he is praying.

Jesus prayed all night and in the early morning, before ministering and after ministering. The Father's ears are open to the prayers of His people regardless of when we pray. Jesus said that we are to pray at all times, and Paul reinforced this teaching when he later wrote that we should *pray without ceasing* (1 Thess. 5:17 KJV).

I once heard an expression that has become a part of my vocabulary: "Continually practice the presence of Jesus." The important thing is that you and I are to give the Lord preeminence in our lives. The Father is not limited to certain hours of the day; He is always attentive to the prayers of His people. He never slumbers or sleeps.

Donnis Griffin, whom I cited as an example of one who prayed early in the morning, was free to adopt this type and time of prayer into her lifestyle. My mother's decision fit into a pattern that suited the lifestyle which she and my dad had chosen for themselves.

It was my husband, Everette, who spoke the words that set me free: "Pressure is not from God. He will not require something of you that applies pressure to you and which then in turn applies pressure to your family, causing everyone to be miserable."

The peace of God which we had enjoyed for many years had been interrupted by my attempt at early morning prayer. That peace was restored when I chose to follow after the Spirit and not after man. Prayer time should be a time of joy in which you gain strength even while praying for others. When you are led by the Spirit in your prayer time, pressures are relieved rather than intensified.

You will have to make a decision to spend time in prayer. Effective praying does require a made-up mind, but it is not attained through sheer willpower. It is an activity which must be motivated by the love of God, for God and for others. It is in your prayer time where human weaknesses are often exposed, but always remember that Jesus said, *My grace is sufficient for thee: for my strength is made perfect in weakness* (2 Cor. 12:9 KJV). You can obey the call to prayer.

Satan would discourage you and steal your time with God, if possible. Ask the Holy Spirit for direction, obey Him, and God's grace will enable you to follow through at your divinely appointed prayer time. You are not sufficient in yourself to think anything of yourself; but your sufficiency is of God (2 Cor. 3:5). It is God's ability in you that will motivate you to a life of prayer. It is His Word that will light your pathway and the Holy Spirit who will take the words of Jesus and reveal them to you.

The disciples asked Jesus to teach them to pray. His teaching in word and practice is our example for prayer today. Do not neglect your time alone with God in Bible study and prayer for this is the key to released power and praying prayers that avail much.

Many people in our Bible studies have listened to various teachers and struggled to pray earlier each morning and to intercede or pray in the Spirit a set number of hours, following the routines of others. It has caused much thanksgiving to God as we have seen these people set free, going from bondage to joy in their prayer time. Whom the Son has set free is free indeed! (John 8:36). Rejoice in your time with the Father—whenever that time may be.

Conclusion:

Conditions for Answered Prayer

*E*veryone who prays desires that his prayers be answered. Some fail to pray because they do not know their spiritual authority and the power of prayer. The laws governing prayer are found in the Scriptures. Obeying them results in answered prayers. These laws are not bondage, but freedom to give and to receive.

The Bible is a revelation of who we are; it establishes our rights and privileges in Christ Jesus. Your particular need is covered in this great Book of the ages. Study the Bible until you are fully persuaded that God will answer your petitions.

> *And this is the confidence that we have in him, that, if we ask any thing according to his will, he heareth us: and if we know that he*

hear us, whatsoever we ask, we know that we have the petitions that we desired of him.

1 John 5:14,15 KJV

Check out your motives regarding your present "need." Is your prayer request made for the good of others or only for self-gratification? Jesus admonished His followers to give. In Luke 6 it is perfectly clear that we will receive according to the measure given, whether it be mercy, judgment, condemnation, forgiveness or material goods. Rid yourself of all selfishness, doing unto others as you would have them do unto you (Luke 6:31). God will answer your prayers if you believe on the name of His Son and love your neighbor as yourself (1 John 3:17-24).

Renew your mind, resisting the temptation to be squeezed into the conceptual mold of this present evil world. After ridding yourself of wrong motives and attitudes, understand that it is God's will to meet your need. Take authority over your thought life. Do not entertain fear or engage in rigidity, denial or emotional isolation. The promised land of rest and peace belonged to the children of Israel, but they failed "to enter therein because of their unbelief" (Heb. 3:19).

Pray According to God's Word

Submit to God and His will, which is recorded in His Word, and all doubts and fears will flee (James 4:7; 1 Peter 5:8,9). James said that a "double-minded" man receives nothing from God. When you ask in faith, without wavering, you will receive "the great recompense of reward"; your prayer will be answered (Heb. 10:19-36).

After you have prayed according to the will and purpose of God, you must cast down every imagination, theory, religious precept, philosophy and reasoning which sets itself against the knowledge of God—His Word (2 Cor. 10:5). Most people have formed patterns of thinking which are contrary to the ways of God. It is your responsibility to bring every thought into captivity, destroying every psychological stronghold with the Gospel of Christ, establishing a new fortress for kingdom living. This means casting aside worry and anxiety about the outcome of that for which you have prayed (1 Peter 5:7; Phil. 4:6).

Refuse to see past mistakes as failures; consider them as stepping-stones which will take you from glory to glory by the Holy Spirit. Circumstances are created through the decision-making process. The Holy Spirit should always guide decisions; however, the results of our choices sometimes conflict with spiritual laws already in motion.

Should you find yourself in a desperate situation, look to God for your deliverance. Believe that God has already delivered you from all your destructions (Ps. 107:20). Through the eye of faith, look at things that are not seen rather than things that are temporal.

Abraham, the father of faith, praised God for the blessing even before it was physically manifested (Rom. 4:20). Praise God for the answer; exercise patience; wait for the answer to your prayer in peace and confidence (Heb. 10:35,36).

Forgiveness—
A Key to Answered Prayer

Jesus said, *"Listen to me! You can pray for anything, and if you believe, you have it; it's yours! But when you are praying, first forgive anyone you are holding a grudge against"* (Mark 11:24,25 TLB). Understanding the process of true forgiveness paves the way for answered prayer. When someone has wronged you, be honest with yourself; express your true feelings and deal truly. Allow the anointing that is upon Jesus to bind up and heal your brokenness. Receive your healing which will enable you to pull down the wall of emotional isolation, permitting others back into your heart. Forgiveness does not always dissipate a memory, but it does eradicate the sting.

An intercessor's prayer life is dependent on having a pure heart and a clear conscience before God. A sincere desire to have a successful prayer life necessitates looking beyond situations, problems and circumstances. Forgive and praise. Call "the things which be not as though they were" (Rom. 4:17). Add patience to your faithful praise, awaiting the answer to your prayer in peace and confidence (Heb. 10:35-37).

Abide in Christ

Jesus reveals the all-inclusive condition of answered prayer in His message to His disciples on the way to the Garden of Gethsemane: *If ye abide in me, and my words abide in you, ye shall ask what ye will, and it shall be done unto you* (John 15:7 KJV). This is an amazing promise that Jesus so boldly makes to us. He gives us this promise, and also prays for us, *that they all may be one; as thou, Father, art in me, and I in thee, that they also may be one in us* (John 17:21 KJV).

This is the key to answered prayer: abiding in Him—the true Vine.

Jesus stated that He is the Vine and we are the branches (John 15:5). The branch standing alone cannot bear fruit, but must receive its life from the vine. Our Lord promised that if we would abide in Him, we would produce fruit—prayer fruit. The fruit of the Spirit is listed in Galatians 5:22-23; here Jesus is speaking of prayer fruit. It is an absolute prerequisite that we abide in the Vine and bear fruit, knowing that without Him we can do nothing.

Many have overlooked one statement that Jesus made in John 15:6. He said that if we do not bear fruit we will be cut off. Prayer is essential to the eternal welfare of each individual believer. Humans have been created for God's pleasure and to bring glory to Him: *Herein is my Father glorified, that ye bear much fruit; so shall ye be my disciples* (John 15:8 KJV).

Jesus said that He came to finish the works of the Father (John 4:34). We must work while it is yet day, for the night is coming when no one can work (John 9:4). We must follow the example of Jesus and finish the work that remains—bearing prayer fruit and preparing the way of the Lord. Be available not only to pray, but also to serve the Father in any area of ministry. A fruit-bearing intercessor is a joyful intercessor.

After Jesus reveals the conditions of answered prayer, He declares the blessings of abiding in Him. One

of those blessings is *joy unspeakable and full of glory.*
(1 Peter 1:8 KJV).

Obey His Commandments

The first prerequisite is that we dwell in God's love
by obeying His commandments (John 15:12-15). Just as
Jesus kept the Father's commandments, so must we. He
assures us that if we abide in the Vine, producing
prayer fruit and obeying the Father, His joy will remain
in us and our joy will be full.

It is impossible to be truly joyful without being truly
loving. That's why the Lord's second injunction is that
we love one another as He has loved us (John 15:12). The
greatest expression of love is the laying down of one's life
for his friends.

Sowing and Reaping

The law of sowing and reaping works in the prayer
arena. There is a time to sow and a time to reap.
*[Remember] this: he who sows sparingly and grudg-
ingly will also reap sparingly and grudgingly, and he
who sows generously [that blessings may come to
someone] will also reap generously and with blessings*
(2 Cor. 9:6).

Don't wait for problems to force you to pray. Be ready for prayer assignments from the Holy Spirit. *Don't be weary in prayer; keep at it; watch for God's answers, and remember to be thankful when they come* (Col. 4:2 TLB). It is in the good times that seed is sown; then when the harvest comes, you will be ready to reap it. When you sow in prayer, God will put you into someone's prayers and you will reap the benefits of someone else's intercession. Without sowing, there will be no reaping.

The liberal person shall be enriched, and he who waters shall himself be watered (Prov. 11:25). Water is a symbol of the Holy Spirit, and as you pray, water will flow out into the desert into the lives of others.

Several years ago my mother, Donnis Griffin, experienced a great trial when she was attacked with a physical illness. Early morning always found her worshiping her heavenly Father and interceding for others as rivers of living water flowed from within her innermost being. As a result, any time she needed to drink from the living water, it was there for her.

The week this problem began, a pastor's wife called me to ask about my mother. She related how an image of Donnis kept coming before her in prayer. God called her to the place of prayer even though she did not know what was happening.

The pain was almost more than my mother could bear, but through the intercession of another she maintained "the good fight of faith" (1 Tim. 6:12). During the first week of this trial, she concealed her pain from those in her household, going right on about her normal activities—cooking meals, taking a neighbor to the hospital, shopping with her week-long visitor and keeping up the solid front of joy. God began to raise up other intercessors to pray for her.

Over the next few weeks, family and friends entered with her into "the good fight of faith." She never wavered in her faith, and God sent forth His Word and healed her (Ps. 107:20).

Sow in season, and you will reap the harvest.

Seek First the Kingdom of God

Seek first the kingdom of God, and His righteousness (Matt. 6:33). God's kingdom is not ushered in with visible signs (Luke 17:20). It is a mystery. The natural human being (the unsaved person) does not receive the things of the Spirit of God, for they are foolishness to him (1 Cor. 2:14). However, I have good news; it has been given to the Christian to know the mystery of the kingdom (Mark 4:11). This knowledge is spiritually discerned.

If you are not praying for your family or your church, begin now. Pray for those who persecute you. Pray for all churches, all denominations, all nations. The more you pray, the more the Holy Spirit will expand your capacity for prayer. Become sensitive to kingdom situations, receiving and cultivating the true intercession of Jesus.

Endnotes

Chapter 1

[1] Strong, James, "Greek," entry #5605, p. 79.

Chapter 2

[1] See "Improving Communication," *Prayers That Avail Much—Volume 1* by Germaine Copeland (Tulsa: Harrison House, 1989), p. 126.

Chapter 3

[1] See "Husbands," *Prayers That Avail Much—Volume 1* by Germaine Copeland (Tulsa: Harrison House, 1989), p. 51.

[2] See "The New Creation Marriage," *Prayers That Avail Much—Volume 2* by Germaine Copeland (Tulsa: Harrison House, 1989, 1991), p. 83.

Chapter 4

[1] Carter, pp. 97, 98.

[2] Goodwin, p. 27.

Chapter 6

[1] See "Adoration: Hallowed Be Thy Name," *Prayers That Avail Much—Volume 2* by Germaine Copeland (Tulsa: Harrison House, 1989, 1991), p. 41.

Chapter 7

[1] Paraphrased excerpt from "To Rejoice in the Lord," *Prayers That Avail Much—Volume 1* by Germaine Copeland (Tulsa: Harrison House, 1989), p. 35.

Chapter 8

[1] Savard, p. 169.
[2] Strong, "Greek," entry #3671, p. 53.
[3] Dake, p. 246.
[4] Vine, p. 257.

Chapter 9

[1] Vine, p. 239.
[2] *Webster,* p. 1351.
[3] *Webster,* p. 1351.
[4] *Webster,* p. 1486.
[5] *Webster,* p. 1486.

References

Carter, Howard. *Questions and Answers on Spiritual Gifts.* Tulsa: Harrison House, 1976.

Dake, Finis Jennings. *Dake's Annotated Reference Bible.* Lawrenceville: Dake Bible Sales, 1963.

Goodwin, J.R. *The Holy Spirit's Three Gifts of Revelation.* Pasadena, Texas: Faith in Depth, Inc., 1974.

Savard, Liberty. *Shattering Your Strongholds.* New Jersey: Bridge-Logos Publishers, 1992. Used by permission.

Strong, James. *Strong's Exhaustive Concordance of the Bible.* "Greek Dictionary of the New Testament." Nashville: Abingdon, 1890.

Vine, W.E. *Vine's Dictionary of Old and New Testament Words.* Old Tappan: Fleming H. Revell, 1981.

Webster's New World Dictionary of American English, Third College Edition. New York: Simon & Schuster, Inc., 1988.

About the Author

Germaine Griffin Copeland, founder and president of Word Ministries, Inc., is the author of the *Prayers That Avail Much* family of books. Her writings provide scriptural prayer instruction to help you pray effectively for those things that concern you and your family and for other prayer assignments. Her teachings on prayer, the personal growth of the intercessor, emotional healing and related subjects have brought understanding, hope, healing and liberty to the discouraged and emotionally wounded. She is a woman of prayer and praise whose highest form of worship is the study of God's Word. Her greatest desire is to know God.

Word Ministries, Inc. is a prayer and teaching ministry. Germaine believes that God has called her to teach the practical application of the Word of Truth for successful, victorious living. After years of searching diligently for truth and trying again and again to come out of depression, she decided that she was a mistake. Out of the depths of despair she called upon the Name of the Lord, and the light of God's presence invaded the room where she was sitting.

It was in that moment that she experienced the warmth of God's love; old things passed away and she felt brand new. She discovered a motivation for living— life had purpose. Living in the presence of God she has found unconditional love and acceptance, healing for crippled emotions, contentment that overcomes depression, peace in the midst of adverse circumstances and grace for developing healthy relationships. The ongoing process of transformation evolved into praying for others, and the prayer of intercession became her prayer focus.

Germaine is the daughter of the Reverend A. H. "Buck" Griffin and the late Donnis Brock Griffin. She and her husband, Everette, have four children, and their prayer assignments increase as more grandchildren and great-grandchildren are born. Germaine and Everette reside in Sandy Springs, a suburb of Atlanta, Georgia.

Word Ministries' offices are located in Historic Roswell, 38 Sloan Street, Roswell, Georgia 30075. Telephone: 770-518-1065.

You may contact
Word Ministries
by writing:

Word Ministries, Inc.
38 Sloan Street
Roswell, Georgia 30075
or calling 770-518-1065
www.prayers.org

*Please include
your testimonies and
praise reports when you write.*

MISSION STATEMENT

Word Ministries, Inc.

To motivate individuals to spiritual growth and emotional wholeness, encouraging them to become more deeply and intimately acquainted with the Father God as they pray prayers that avail much.

Other Books by Germaine Copeland

The Road God Walks

Prayers That Avail Much® Journal

Prayers That Avail Much® Commemorative Gift Edition

*Prayers That Avail Much® Commemorative
Leather Edition*

*Prayers That Avail Much® for Business
Executive Edition*

Prayers That Avail Much®—Volume 1

Prayers That Avail Much®—Volume 1
(Mass Market Edition)

Prayers That Avail Much®—Volume 2

Prayers That Avail Much®—Volume 2
(Mass Market Edition)

Prayers That Avail Much®—Volume 3

Prayers That Avail Much®—Volume 3
(Mass Market Edition)

Prayers That Avail Much® Journal

Prayers That Avail Much® for Men
(Clothbound)

Prayers That Avail Much® for Women
(Clothbound)

Prayers That Avail Much® for Mothers
(Clothbound)

Prayers That Avail Much® for Mothers
(Paperback)

Prayers That Avail Much® for Teens
(Clothbound)

Prayers That Avail Much® for Kids

Prayers That Avail Much® for Kids—Book 2

Prayers That Avail Much® for the Workplace

Oraciones Con Poder—Prayers That Avail Much®
(Spanish Edition)

Available from your local bookstore.

Harrison House
Tulsa, OK 74153

The Harrison House Vision

Proclaiming the truth and the power

Of the Gospel of Jesus Christ

With excellence;

Challenging Christians to

Live victoriously,

Grow spiritually,

Know God intimately.